Criminal Justice
Recent Scholarship

Edited by
Marilyn McShane and Frank P. Williams III

A Series from LFB Scholarly

School Community and Disorder
Communal Schools, Student Bonding, Delinquency, and Victimization

Allison Ann Payne

LFB Scholarly Publishing LLC
New York 2004

Copyright © 2004 by LFB Scholarly Publishing LLC

Library of Congress Cataloging-in-Publication Data

Payne, Allison Ann, 1975-
  School community and disorder : communal schools, student bonding,
delinquency, and victimization / Allison Ann Payne.
      p. cm. -- (Criminal justice)
  Includes bibliographical references and index.
  ISBN 1-59332-042-6 (alk. paper)
  1. School violence--United States--Prevention. 2. School
environment--United States. 3. Social control--United States. I. Title.
II. Series: Criminal justice (LFB Scholarly Publishing LLC)
  LB3013.32.P39 2004
  371.7'82--dc22

2004006938

ISBN 1-59332-042-6

Printed on acid-free 250-year-life paper.

Manufactured in the United States of America.

For Steve, with all that I am

TABLE OF CONTENTS

List of Tables...xi

List of Figures...xv

Chapter 1: Introduction...1

Chapter 2: Communal School Organization and Student Bonding:
Previous Research...7

Social Organization of Schools...7

Communal School Organization...10

Student Bonding..23

The Links..29

Interactions...30

Hypotheses Examined..31

Chapter 3: Study Data and Measures 33

Data..33

Final Sample...41

Measures...43

Plans for Analysis...68

Chapter 4: Relationships among Communal School Organization,
Student Bonding, and School Disorder: Study Results 79

Measurement Models...79

Control Variables...83

Hypothesis 1..86

Hypothesis 2..……...90

Hypothesis 3..93

Chapter 5: Intearctions among Communal School Organization,
School Size, and Racial Diversity 97

Hypothesis 4..97

Chanpter 6: Discussion...119

Summary of Findings..119

Discussion of Findings..121

Limitations of Study...125

Future Research..128

Potential for Prevention..131

Conclusion..134

References..137

Index..149

LIST OF TABLES

Table 1: Response Rate Details for Principal Surveys.....................34

Table 2: Response Rate Details for Phase Two Surveys...............36

Table 3: Correlations of School/Community Characteristics with Participation...39

Table 4: Original Scales and Sources for Scales used in Study.........44

Table 5: Operationalization of Communal School Organization.......45

Table 6: Factor Analysis of Communal School Organization items...48

Table 7: Correlations among the Components of Communal School Organization...49

Table 8: Operationalization of Student Bonding.........................50

Table 9: Factor Analysis of Student Bonding items.....................53

Table 10: Correlations among the Components of Student Bonding...54

Table 11: Operationalization of School Disorder.........................56

Table 12: Factor Analysis of School Disorder items.....................60

Table 13: Correlations among the Components of School Disorder..61

Table 14: Correlations among the School Disorder Components and other Measures of School Disorder.............................62

Table 15: Means, Standard Deviations, and Ranges for Control Variables..63

Table 16: Correlations among the Control Variables....................64

Table 17: Racial Distribution of Student Body and Faculty.............65

Table 18: Correlations between Student Racial Percentages and the Variables of Interest...66

Table 19: Correlations of Control Variables with the Variables of Interest...84

Table 20: Standardized Regression Coefficients for Control Variables on the Variables of Interest...............................85

Table 21: Standardized Regression Coefficients for School Disorder on Interaction Terms..98

Table 22: Standardized Regression Coefficients for Delinquency on Interaction Terms...99

Table 23: Standardized Regression Coefficients for Teacher Victimization on Interaction Terms.............................100

Table 24: Standardized Regression Coefficients for Student Victimization on Interaction Terms.............................101

Table 25: Regression Coefficients for School Disorder on Interaction between Communal School Organization and Teacher Racial Heterogeneity with Communal School Organization split at the 50th percentile............................103

Table 26: Regression Coefficients for School Disorder on Interaction between Communal School Organization and Teacher Racial Heterogeneity with Teacher Racial Heterogeneity split at the 50th percentile...........................105

Table 27: Regression Coefficients for Teacher Victimization on Interaction between Communal School Organization and Teacher Racial Heterogeneity with   Communal School Organization split at the 50th percentile............................106

Table 28: Regression Coefficients for Teacher Victimization on Interaction between Communal School Organization and Teacher Racial Heterogeneity with Teacher Racial Heterogeneity split at the 50th percentile...........................107

Table 29: Regression Coefficients for School Disorder on Interaction between Communal School Organization and Student Racial Heterogeneity with Communal School Organization split at the 50th percentile............................109

Table 30: Regression Coefficients for School Disorder on Interaction between Communal School Organization and Student Racial Heterogeneity with Student Racial Heterogeneity split at the 50th percentile...........................110

Table 31: Regression Coefficients for Delinquency on Interaction between Communal School Organization and Student/ Teacher Ratio with Communal School Organization split at the 50th percentile...111

Table 32: Regression Coefficients for Delinquency on Interaction between Communal School Organization and Student/ Teacher Ratio with Student/Teacher Ratio split at the 50th percentile...113

Table 33: Regression Coefficients for Delinquency on Interaction between Communal School Organization and Student/ Teacher Ratio with Communal School Organization split at the 50th percentile, alternative schools removed.................114

Table 34: Regression Coefficients for Student Victimization on Interaction between Communal School Organization and Student Enrollment with Communal School Organization split at the 50th percentile...115

Table 35: Regression Coefficients for Student Victimization on Interaction between Communal School Organization and Student Enrollment with Student Enrollment split at the 50th percentile..116

LIST OF FIGURES

Figure 1: Model Estimated for Hypothesis One..................73

Figure 2: Model Estimated for Hypothesis Two...................74

Figure 3: Model Estimated for Hypothesis Three.................75

Figure 4: Measurement Model for Communal School Organization...80

Figure 5: Measurement Model for Student Bonding...............81

Figure 6: Measurement Model for School Disorder..............82

Figure 7: Results for Model Estimated for Hypothesis One
(First Estimation)......................................87

Figure 8: Results for Model Estimated for Hypothesis Two
(Second Estimation).....................................88

Figure 9: Results for Model Estimated for Hypothesis Two............91

Figure 10: Results for Model Estimated for Hypothsis Three
(First Estimation)..92

Figure 11: Results for Model Estimated for Hypothesis Three
(Second Estimation).....................................95

xiii

ACKNOWLEDGEMENTS

First and foremost, many thanks goes to Gary and Denise Gottfredson for the very generous use of the National Study of Delinquency Prevention in Schools data. I would also like to thank Denise Gottfredson for her incredible guidance and support over the years, John H. Laub, Gary LaFree, Sylvia Rosenfield, and Doug Smith for their helpful comments and suggestions, and Leo Balk for his help in the editorial realm. Finally, I would like to thank Steve for his constant support.

CHAPTER 1

Introduction

Over the past decade, violence and crime in schools has emerged as a dominant concern of the public in general, and of educators and criminologists more specifically. A recent poll reported that 60% of Americans believe school crime is increasing (Brooks, Schiraldi, and Ziedenberg, 2000). The same survey reported a 49% increase in people who feared a school shooting would occur in their neighborhood (Brooks et al., 2000).

Recent statistics, however, suggest that this fear of increasing school crime and violence is not justified. The National School Safety Center (2001) reported that school-related deaths decreased 50% between the 1992-1993 school year and the 2000-2001 school year, from 56 to 23. Bureau of Justice Statistics and the U.S. Department of Education (Kaufman, Chen, Choy, Peter, Ruddy, Miller, Fleury, Chandler, Planty, and Rand, 2001) reported that violent victimizations in schools declined from 48 per 1000 students in 1992 to 43 per 1000 students in 1998. Similarly, the percentage of students who were victims of a crime declined from 10% in 1995 to 8% in 1999 (Kaufman et al., 2001). Overall school crime showed a decrease of almost one-third from 144 per 1000 in 1992 to 101 per 1000 in 1998 (Kaufman et al., 2001). The same report showed a decline in the percentage of students carrying weapons to school, from 12% in 1993 to 7% in 1999, and a decline in the percentage of students reporting the presence of gangs in their school, from 29% in 1995 to 17% in 1999 (Kaufman et al., 2001).

While school violence is less frequent than believed by the general public, serious forms of delinquency and victimization in schools are still a problem. In a 1998 national survey of delinquency in schools, 6.7% of school principals reported at least one physical attack or fight involving a weapon in their schools, while 37.3% of secondary school students reported having hit or threatened to hit other students in the past year (G. Gottfredson, D. Gottfredson, Czeh, Cantor, Crosse, and Hantman, 2000). In the same study, 19% of students reported having been threatened, 14% reported having been attacked, and 5% reported having been threatened with a knife or a gun. Similarly, 20% of teachers reported being threatened, although only 3% reported actually being attacked (G. Gottfredson et al., 2000).

Even more common are incidents of less serious delinquency and victimization. In the study mentioned above, 28% of teachers reported damage to property worth less than $10, 24% reported theft of property worth less than $10, 14% reported damage to property worth more than $10, and 13% reported theft of property worth more than $10 (G. Gottfredson et al., 2000). Similarly, 16% of secondary school students reported damaging or destroying school property and 9% report engaging in theft.

Aside from the obvious costs of school crime on property damage and loss and personal injury, school disorder is costly because it reduces the ability of schools to carry out their educational mission. Surveys of American teachers (e.g., Harris, Louis, and Associates, 1993) document some of school disorder's collateral effects on the learning environment. These surveys show that the threat of school violence results in lower teacher and student attendance at school. Teachers in disorderly schools also spend a large proportion of their time coping with behavior problems rather than in academic instruction, which results in lower levels of academic engagement, academic performance, and eventually graduation rates. Fear of victimization in schools has also been shown to influence students' ability to concentrate and learn (Lawrence, 1998; McDermott, 1980). Finally, disorder is likely to influence the schooling experience more generally by affecting staffing quality. A recent analysis of data collected by the National Center for Education Statistics (Ingersoll, 2001) showed higher teacher turnover in schools with greater discipline problems, and teachers cited discipline problems as a major reason for leaving. These problems are especially severe in urban areas.

It is clear that it is in the best interests of students, teachers, and the general public to focus efforts within schools on reducing school disorder. Schools are a logical location for delinquency prevention activities, since most youth attend school on a regular basis and view school as the normal place for these types of activities (D. Gottfredson, 2001). Schools present the opportunity for affecting youth's knowledge, attitudes, norms, and skills (Botvin, Schinke, and Orlandi, 1995). In addition, research has identified many factors related to school that are predictive of delinquency. At the school-level, the availability of criminogenic commodities within the school, the social organization of the school, and the emotional climate of the school have all been found to predict student delinquency (D. Gottfredson, Wilson, and Najaka, 2002). School-related individual-level predictors of delinquency include school performance, attendance, and student bonding to school (D. Gottfredson et al., 2002). School-based programs that target these factors are likely to be effective at reducing school delinquency and problem behavior.

Although research has identified both school-level and individual-level predictors of delinquency, the majority of programs and prevention efforts found in schools are targeted at individual students and the majority of research conducted on school-based prevention focuses on these individually-directed interventions. When compiling studies of school-based interventions, D. Gottfredson et a. (2002) found that a greater percentage of studies focused on individual-level interventions, such as prevention curriculum or cognitive training, rather than school-level interventions, such as norm establishment or school capacity building. Prevention curricula, which generally focus on teaching students factual information about the dangers of problem behavior or skills to resist engaging in this behavior, were the main strategies examined in 81% of the studies, while cognitive or behavioral training was the main strategy examined in 64% of the studies, as opposed to norm establishment (30% of the studies) and school and discipline management (12% of the studies).

As is evident, research on school disorder and prevention has somewhat lacked a focus on school-level characteristics, especially when compared with the focus on individual student characteristics. This is in contrast, however, to theorizing about the causes of crime. Several criminological theories propose aggregate-level explanations of crime and delinquency. Most relevant to this research is Sampson's concept of neighborhood collective efficacy (Morenoff, Sampson, and Raudenbush, 2001; Sampson, Morenoff, and Earls, 1997; Sampson, Raudenbush, and Earls, 1999). Collective efficacy is considered the opposite of social disorganization, as defined by Shaw and McKay (1972), and refers to positive social relations among neighbors in a community as well as the willingness of neighbors to intervene for the good of the community (Sampson et al., 1997). Collective efficacy "highlights shared expectations and mutual engagement by residents in local social control" (Morenoff et al., 2001:520) Sampson proposes that neighborhoods differ in their levels of collective efficacy, and neighborhoods with higher collective efficacy levels will have higher levels of informal social control, defined as the capacity of a community to regulate the behavior of its members. These higher levels of social control will then lead to lower levels of crime and delinquency. Sampson and his colleagues have found support for the hypotheses (Sampson et al., 1997; Sampson et al., 1999; Sampson and Raudenbush, 1999).

This idea of the collective efficacy of a neighborhood can be applied quite easily to schools. As mentioned above, the social organization of the school is a predictor of student delinquency. Research has illustrated the importance of school social organization in general, and specifically the importance of communal school organization (Bryk and Driscoll, 1988; D. Gottfredson, 2001). Communal school organization refers to the organization of a school as a community and includes supportive relationships between and among teachers, administrators, and students, a common set of goals and norms, and a sense of collaboration and involvement, concepts that are clearly related to collective efficacy. It is has been shown that schools which are communally organized have more positive student attitudes, better teacher morale, and less student problem behavior (Bryk and Driscoll, 1988; Battistich, Solomon, Kim, Watson, and Schaps, 1995; Battistich and Hom, 1997).

Drawing again from Sampson's work, it is natural to suggest that communal schools will have better informal social control, thereby having students who are more bonded to the school. Student bonding has already been mentioned as another important predictor of delinquency. As described by Hirschi (1969), the student bond is the link between the student and the school which restrains the student from delinquency because he or she values the bond and does not want to damage it. Hirschi's control theory assumes that when a student's bond to school is weakened or broken, that student is much more likely to engage in delinquency. The importance of student bonding and its effect on student achievement and problem behavior is supported by research (Krohn and Massey, 1980; Liska and Reed, 1985; Agnew, 1985; Thornberry, Lizotte, Krohn, Farnworth, and Jang, 1991; Cernkovich and Giordano, 1992; Jenkins, 1997; Welsh et al., 1999; Gottfredson, et al., 2000).

This study focuses on the school-level relationships between communal school organization, student bonding, and school disorder. It is hypothesized that schools that are more communally organized will have students who are more bonded to school and, therefore, have lower levels of delinquency and victimization. Structural equation models were created representing these relationships, and LISREL (version 7.16; Joreskog and Sorbom, 1989) was used to analyze these models. This study also examines the effect of interactions between communal school organization and two controls variables, racial heterogeneity and school size, on school disorder. It is hypothesized that communal school organization will have a stronger effect on school disorder in larger schools and schools that are more racially heterogeneous. Chapter 2 presents a review of the literature relevant to these concepts while Chapter 3 provides information on the data set, measures, and models used in this research. Chapters 4 and 5 present the results of the analyses and Chapter 6 is a discussion of these results.

Communal School Organization and Student Bonding: Previous Research

SOCIAL ORGANIZATION OF SCHOOLS

The very basis of this research rests on the importance of the social organization of a school. Waller (1932) presented the idea of a school as an organization that includes not only a formal structure but a system of social relations as well. According to Waller (1932), this system of social relations, the social organization of the school, has an effect on the workings of the school that is as significant as that of the formal structure.

The social relations in a school, the cultural system of values and norms, the management structure, and the interactions between and among faculty, administrators, and students, all have great influence of the success of a school. For example, studies show that a school's social organization predicts the level of disorder in the school (D. Gottfredson, 1987; G. Gottfredson and D. Gottfredson, 1985; D. Gottfredson, G. Gottfredson, and Hybl, 1993). Schools with good teacher-administration communication, high levels of planning, and effective problem-solving methods tend to have higher teacher morale and less disorder. G. Gottfredson and D. Gottfredson (1985) found that schools in which teachers and administrators displayed high levels of cooperation and students perceived rules to be clear and fairly enforced experienced lower levels of teacher and student victimization. Similarly, schools that have a system of shared values and expectations and that experience meaningful social interactions also have less disorder (Duke, 1989). Finally, schools in which the students have a high sense of belonging experience lower levels of disorder (Duke, 1989). G. Gottfredson (1987) presented similar findings on disorderly schools: Teachers in a disorderly school tend to have lower morale and poor perception of the school's administration. They also report a lack of support, planning, and action for school improvement activities.

More support for the importance of a school's social organization can be found in studies on effective schools conducted over the past two decades. For instance, Fullan (1985) discussed the organizational characteristics of an effective school, which include orderly climates, clear organizational goals, and high expectations for students. Purkey and Smith (1983) also acknowledged the importance of the organizational characteristics of a school. They discussed how the norms, rituals, and values of a school combine to create the climate of the school, which forms the basis of the school's culture that is the key to an effective school.

Lieberman and Miller (1984) also discussed the importance of the school culture. The authors defined school culture as the informal norms that develop out of the regular routine of school life, primarily the work life of the teachers. As teachers and administrators talk about their work, as they plan and prepare together, as they observe each other, a special culture emerges. This culture includes strong support, high levels of trust, a caring ethos, and high levels of staff collegiality. All of these characteristics create a positive climate that can have positive effects on the students.

Corcoran (1985) discussed the ways in which organizational factors in a school affect academic and behavioral student outcomes. He suggested that positive and collaborative relationships among teachers and between teachers and administrators effects the success of a school, and that the nature of these relationships has more to do with the school's success than any other factor, including the make-up of the student population. Corcoran also suggested that the work norms of a school are more important than the actual work practices. What is necessary is a school climate that assimilates the school's practices and policies into an overall community of caring people. This community contains certain norms that are essential for the school to be successful, including high levels of trust, expectations, cooperation, collegiality, effort, and respect, as well as a belief in school improvement and a sense of collective responsibility. According to Corcoran, these norms are often embedded in the rules and regulations of the school. However, the fact that members of the school accept and adhere to the norms is due less to the specific policies and procedures and more to the overall climate and culture of the school. A strong school culture provides a core set of assumptions and understandings that govern behavior. It also creates a sense of social cohesion among school personnel, thereby providing both support and direction.

Welsh, Greene, and Jenkins (1999) discussed how the social organization of a school includes unwritten beliefs, values, and attitudes that greatly influence the interaction among all school members. According to Welsh et al. (1999), the social organization of the school can be described as the "feel of the workplace as perceived by those who work or attend school there" (p. 79). This climate includes communication patterns, behavior norms, reward and sanction systems, and role structures, and sets the boundaries for acceptable behavior for students, teachers, and administrators.

Finally, Lee, Bryk, and Smith (1992) discussed school social organization, which they defined as the structure of social relations within the school. According to the authors, a discussion of school social organization includes the following questions: "How do teachers interact with one another?", "What relationships do they maintain with students?", and "How do these sets of relations affect how schools work and how teachers and students work within them?" Based on these questions, the social organization of a school involves two distinct groups of people in the school: the adults (teachers, administrators, and other staff) and the students. The relationships within these groups, the collegiality among the teachers and the peer relations among the students, are extremely important to the effectiveness of the school. As important to the school's effectiveness are the relationships across these groups, the ties between teachers and students. These affective bonds among and between teachers, administrators, and students are crucial to the success of the school.

An important aspect of the social organization of the school, as discussed by Lee et al. (1992), is the cultural system of the school, defined as the system of values and norms in the school. Included in this culture are norms for instruction, which affect the way teachers teach and students learn and include beliefs about students' learning abilities and acceptable student and teacher classroom behavior. Also included in this culture are norms for civility, which affect the relations among school members and include beliefs about the way to treat others within the school. The norms for civility exhibited in effective schools include concern for the welfare of others within the school. Norms such as these can result in positive consequences for both teachers and students.

Another important aspect of school social organization, as discussed by Lee et al. (1992), are the collegial ties among the faculty. There is both a formal and informal side to this collegiality. On the formal side, collegiality promotes communication of expertise; that is, teachers share practices and strategies with other teachers. On the informal side, collegiality promotes a friendly social environment in the school; that is, teachers spend time with other teachers and enjoy being in the school. These two sides of faculty collegiality are, of course, intertwined. Teachers who work in a school characterized by a positive social environment are more likely to be receptive to other teachers' ideas and are more likely to share their own ideas. Thus, this collegiality provides teachers with personal relationships, encouragement, and knowledge, all of which can reduce a teacher's sense of isolation and vulnerability.

COMMUNAL SCHOOL ORGANIZATION

Lee et al. (1992) discussed two distinct perspectives of school organization. The Rational-Bureaucratic Perspective views the school as a formal organization in which there is a strict division of adult labor as defined by the teachers' subject matters. Interactions within this type of organization mainly deal with technical knowledge and are characterized by little individual discretion. A Rational-Bureaucratic school strives to efficiently serve a large number of students whose backgrounds and interests are diverse and tends to have a complex set of organizational goals and a large administrative staff whose social relations are of a limited nature.

A second perspective of school organization discussed by Lee et al. (1992) is the Personal-Communal Perspective. This perspective sees a school as a small society, as an organization that is lead by a common ethos and emphasizes informal social relationships. As opposed to a Rational-Bureaucratic school, the adult labor in a Personal-Communal school is not strictly divided and the teacher role is extremely diverse. Social relations within this type of school are more personal in nature and are of the utmost importance for both the teachers and the students. The organizational goals of the school are less complex and common norms and experiences are emphasized.

It is this communal school organization that will be the focus of this research. As defined by Solomon, Battistich, Kim, and Watson (1997), a school that is communally organized, that has a high sense of community, is one in which "...members know, care about, and support one another, have common goals and sense of shared purpose, and to which they actively contribute and feel personally committed." (Solomon et al., 1997, p. 236)

The idea of "the school as a community" has been in existence for at least half of a century. Dewey (1966) viewed a student's educational experience as a social process and the school as a community that was designed to promote this social process. The following quote of his best illustrate these ideas: "The school must itself be a community life in all which that implies. Social perceptions and interests can be developed only in a genuinely social medium – one where there is give and take in the building up of common experience...Much of present education fails because it neglects this fundamental principle of the school as a form of community life." (p. 358)

Corcoran (1985) also discussed the importance of this sense of community within schools. In many schools, teachers feel isolated and lonely; they feel as though they are held in low esteem and that they receive little support from others. These feelings are stressful obstacles that inhibit teacher productivity. Corcoran declared that the reverse is true in effective schools: teachers feel respected, relationships are supportive and reciprocal, and the sense of community is strong. Within these communal schools, there exists a shared system of beliefs, values, and goals, and the management structure is based on consensus rather than hierarchy.

McMillan and Chavis (1986) described sense of community as the "feeling that members have of belonging, a feeling that members matter to one another and to the group, and a shared faith that members' needs will be met through the commitment to be together" (p. 9). Included in this sense of community is the concept of membership, which is the sense that a person belongs to the community, and the concept of influence, which is the feeling that the person matters to the community and that the community matters to the person. Also included is the concept of reinforcement, that some need or needs of the person are being met through the community; this involves the idea that members of the community share a set of values, needs, priorities, and goals that are satisfied through the community. Finally, sense of community includes a shared emotional connection, which comes from a commitment, history, and experiences that are common to the members of the community.

Battistich and his colleagues (Solomon, Watson, Battistich, Schaps, and Delucchi, 1992; Battistich, Solomon, Kim, Watson, and Schaps, 1995; Battistich, Schaps, Watson, and Solomon, 1996; Battistich and Solomon, 1997; Solomon, Battistich, Kim, and Watson, 1997; Battistich and Hom, 1997) have also agreed that the view of a school as a community is a powerful framework for examining educational practices and educational reform and can help schools be more effective in meeting the needs of both teachers and students. However, they recognized that there is no agreed-upon definition of school community or communal school organization. Most researchers have agreed that a communal school is one in which members in the school care about each other and support each other, members feel as though they belong to the school community, members share common norms, values, and goals, and members participate in and influence the community's activities. However, differences in definitions do exist. Some researchers have focused more on the feeling of belonging people get from community membership (Goodenow 1993a, 1993b), while others have focused on both belonging and participation (Solomon et al., 1997). Some researchers have examined the school community from the perspectives of the teachers (Bryk and Driscoll, 1988; Lee, Bryk, and Smith, 1992), some from that of the students (Solomon et al., 1992; Battistich et al., 1995), and some from the perspectives of both teachers and students (Battistich et al., 1997).

Most researchers have agreed, however, that a communal school meets the needs of both teachers and students, who therefore become bonded with other school community members and committed to the school's mission and goals, and are then more likely to internalize the school's norms and rules (Battistich et al., 1997). Essentially, because the relationships that develop among members in a communal school are more caring and supportive and because the planning and decision making that occurs in a communal school are influenced by all members, members in a communal school develop a high sense of belonging and a common set of goals.

Much educational research has demonstrated the importance of different aspects of the communal school concept without specifically discussing the school as a community (Bryk and Driscoll, 1988; Solomon et al., 1997). For instance, researchers have highlighted the importance of a common purpose and a set of shared values among the teachers and administrators in order to have a successful school (Rutter, Maughan, Mortimore, Outson, and Smith, 1979; Grant and Capell, 1983). Others have found that supportive school environments which promote supportive relationships between teachers and students can protect those students from high-risk behavior (Werner and Smith, 1992; Zimmerman and Arunkumar, 1994). Other research supports the findings of the importance of supportive teachers and personalized teacher-student relationships (McLaughlin, 1990; Schwartz, Merten, and Bursik, 1987). Goodenow (1993a, 1993b) found support for the influence of students' feelings of belonging and their academic achievement and school attendance.

Fullan and Hargreaves (1996) discussed how a collaborative school culture is more effective than the individualistic culture that characterizes most schools. In an individualistic culture, teachers work alone and are not able to get important feedback from their colleagues. In a collaborative culture, however, teachers share responsibility and commitment to the students and the school, and are able to improve and work far more effectively (Fullan and Hargreaves, 1996).

Support for certain aspects of communal school organization can also be seen in the research underlying the KEYS (Keys to Excellence in Your Schools) program (Hawley and Rollie, 2002). Based on research showing how changes to the culture and organization of a school can improve the school's effectiveness, the KEYS program works to increase collegiality, collective action, and collaboration in a school through six KEYS for improvement. Two of these KEYS directly relate to communal school organization: (1) Shared understanding and commitment to high goals, and (2) open communication and collaborative problem-solving. Much research illustrates the importance of shared commitment and collaboration (Hawley and Rollie, 2002). For instance, Little (1990) and Louis, Marks, and Kruse (1993) found that teachers' shared sense of support and responsibility is increased by collaboration. Additionally, Kruse, Louis, and Bryk (1995) found that two important elements of effective teaching communities are shared values and collaboration, while Newmann and Wehlage (1995) found that staff collegiality and collaboration greatly influences the effectiveness of a school.

Educational research has also demonstrated the benefits of overall communal school organization. Membership in a school community has many positive consequences for teachers: it can result in a reduction of teacher isolation and an increase of teacher supportiveness (Little, 1985; Bird and Little, 1986), teacher satisfaction, and teacher self-efficacy (Bryk and Driscoll, 1988). Membership also has positive consequences for students: it can increase student achievement, motivation, and school attachment (Newmann, 1981; Battistich et al., 1995), reduce student problem behavior and alienation (Battistich et al., 1995; Battistich and Hom, 1997).

A study by Newmann, Rutter, and Smith (1989) provided additional support for the importance of a sense of community within a school. According to the researchers, a high sense of community is indicated by teachers' perceptions that other teachers hold the same values and goals and that there is a sense of supportiveness and mutual respect among teachers. This consensus on the goals of the school and the sense of supportiveness that derives from the communal nature of the schools make teachers more effective and increases student achievement. After examining organizational features in 353 public high schools, they found that these communal school features had a major influence on teachers' views of the school climate, and on teacher efficacy, communication, and expectations. Increases in the unity of the faculty, in teacher sense of belonging, and in cooperative interdependence of teachers counteracted the work fragmentation and social isolation felt by these teachers. The authors concluded, therefore, that improving the sense of community in the school can reduce teacher alienation and improve teachers' views of the school climate.

Newmann (1996) continued his examination on the importance of a school community by looking at how the school's social organization can be changed to increase both the academic and social success of its students. In order for the students to be successful, the teachers must be able to work together as best as possible; they must be able to function well as a unit. In order to achieve this, the school must be organized as a community with a clear and common purpose and diverse opportunities for teacher collaboration. Schools that have strong communities will be better able to function and will have more successful teachers and students (Newmann, 1996).

Bryk and his colleagues (Bryk, 1995; Bryk and Driscoll, 1988; Bryk and Thum, 1989; Lee, Bryk, and Smith, 1992) also presented much discussion and research on the concept of communal school organization. They characterized a communal school as a social organization which exhibits cooperative relations among adults, a common purpose, and a daily routine that fosters commitment among its members. The adults in this type of school are greatly committed to the organization due to their engagement in a common mission and a network of supportive relationships. It is the elements of a communal school, the cooperation, communication, and common goals, that make the school successful.

Bryk and Driscoll (1988) argued that three core ideas make up the overall concept of communal school organization: a system of shared values, a common agenda, and an ethos of caring. According to the researchers, these three elements combine in a communal school and demonstrate powerful effects on all members of the school community.

The first element of communal school organization, as proposed by Bryk and Driscoll (1988), is a system of shared values. These are ideas about the mission and goals of the school, how teachers and administrators should behave, how students should behave, and how and what students should learn. This system is created when interactions among the faculty result in a shared purpose and a common language about work. This system of common values and norms is shown through the community members' behavior, such as the educational practices of the teachers, the ways in which discipline problems are handled, and the concern for others that is shown by all members. These behaviors, which arise when members of a communal school internalize the shared values and norms, support the mission and goals of the overall school. What is important about this system of shared values is not only that they exist, but that they are internalized and embraced by all members of the school community (Bryk and Driscoll, 1988).

A common agenda of activities is the second element of communal school organization. These activities range from academic classes, to informal interaction between and among students and teachers, to formal school-wide activities such as dances or sporting events. This common agenda provides opportunities for members of the communal school to interact with each other and participate in shared experiences, thereby encouraging members to get to know each other and to internalize the shared system of norms and values (Bryk, 1995). Through these interactions, teachers and students are able to foster meaningful relationships that increase both parties' attachment to the school community and its members (Bryk and Driscoll, 1988).

The third element of communal school organization is an ethos of caring embodied in the social relations found in the school. This ethos is seen in the collegial nature of the relations among the adults in the school as well as in the broad role teachers fulfill in the school. The first important aspect of the ethos of caring is teacher collegiality, which is manifested in the esteem and respect teachers hold for one another. This collegiality has both academic and social results. Academically, it means that teachers engage in a collaborative problem-solving process by providing help for each other and planning activities together. Because of this, the decision-making that occurs in the school is characterized by less conflict and more trust (Bryk, 1995). Socially, it means that teachers engage in personal relationships with each other, including spending time with colleagues outside of school. Because of the collegial relations between members of the faculty, teachers are more likely to view the school as a friendly environment in which they can gain satisfaction. The second important aspect of the ethos of caring is a diffuse teacher role. This means that teacher responsibilities extend beyond the classroom to include non-classroom interactions with students. Through these interactions, teachers focus on enhancing both the academic and personal development of students (Bryk and Driscoll, 1988).

According to Bryk and Driscoll (1988), communal school organization has consequences for both teachers and students.

Teachers are more likely to be satisfied with their work, to be seen as enjoying their work, to have high morale, and to have lower number of absences. Because the teachers are happier in a communal school, they will have more positive interactions with the students. These interactions will result in more student attachment to the school, which will result in positive consequences for the students. Students in a communal school are less likely to misbehave and to dropout of school, and more likely to be interested in academics and to have higher academic achievement.

Bryk and Driscoll (1988) presented several specific hypotheses regarding communal school organization. They hypothesized that teachers in a communal school will be more likely to have high levels of self-efficacy, satisfaction, work enjoyment, and morale and low levels of alienation and absenteeism. They also hypothesized that students in a communal school will have lower levels of misbehavior, alienation, truancy, and absenteeism, and higher levels academic achievement.

Bryk and Driscoll (1988) tested their hypotheses using a subset of 357 schools from the High School and Beyond data. They used data from principal and student questionnaires from 1980 and 1982 and teacher and principal questionnaires from 1984. While not all constructs of communal school organization are well measured in the data, such as the specific content of the norms in the schools, the study does have the advantage of using data from a large, nationally representative data set with multiple sources.

After examining zero-order correlations, the researchers found results that followed the expected patterns (Bryk and Driscoll, 1988). Levels of teacher efficacy, work enjoyment, and morale were higher and teacher absenteeism was lower in schools that were communally organized. These schools also had lower levels of student misbehavior and dropouts, and higher levels of academic interest and math achievement.

Similar results were found when the researchers estimated Hierarchical Linear Regression Models (Bryk and Driscoll, 1988). After controlling for factors such as school size, social class, and student composition, the communal school index demonstrated a powerful effect on teacher and student outcomes. Communal school organization explained 25.3% of teacher efficacy and satisfaction variance and had a coefficient that was four times larger than any other in the equation. Similarly, the communal index explained 14.7% of teacher work enjoyment and had a coefficient five times larger than any other. Communal school organization also had a significant effect on staff morale and teacher absenteeism.

Similar patterns were found for student outcomes (Bryk and Driscoll, 1988). Communal school organization had a significant negative effect on class cutting, student absenteeism, classroom disorder, and dropout rates; the communal index coefficient was the largest in each of these equations. Students in communally organized schools also experienced higher levels of academic interest and achievement.

Bryk and Driscoll (1988) also explored school-related factors that facilitate the creation and sustenance of communal school organization. They hypothesized that smaller schools are more likely to be communally organized, due to the bureaucratic nature often found in larger schools. As discussed previously, this rational-bureaucratic outlook is in direct opposition to the communal outlook. Therefore, Bryk and Driscoll (1988) anticipated that school size would negatively influence communal school organization.

The researchers also hypothesized that student racial and ethnic heterogeneity would be inversely related to communal school organization, based on the existence of shared beliefs and values in a communal school. Because homogeneity facilitates the development of these shared values, heterogeneity would make the creation of a communal organization more difficult (Bryk and Driscoll, 1988).

Both hypotheses regarding factors facilitating the sustenance of communal school organization were supported. Smaller schools were more likely to be communally organized. In addition, communal school organization was less common in schools with more racially heterogeneous student bodies, although the strength of this effect was relatively weak.

D. Gottfredson (2001) discussed how Bryk's concept of communal school organization relates to student delinquency. Schools that are organized as a community, those that are characterized by shared values, positive social interactions, an ethos of caring, and extended teacher roles, are more likely to have low levels of delinquency. This is because delinquent norms are unable to survive in the normative climate that develops in a communal school. Because of the system of shared values and the positive social interactions between teachers and students, delinquent norms are weakened. Conversely, in schools that are not socially organized as a community, delinquent norms can survive and even flourish, thus leading to higher levels of student delinquency (D. Gottfredson, 2001).

Battistich and his colleagues (Solomon et al., 1992; Battistich et al., 1995; Battistich et al., 1996; Battistich and Hom, 1997; Battistich et al., 1997) have also conducted research in the area of communal school organization, which they describe as the existence of a "caring community" within the school. A caring school is one characterized by concern and support for and respect among its members (Solomon et al., 1992). Members feel as though they belong, as though they are respected and valued, and as though they make meaningful contributions to the community (Battistich et al., 1995). This leads members to feel committed to and responsible for the community and to want to uphold the norms shared by all (Solomon et al., 1992).

Battistich and his colleagues have examined the effects of communal school organization on student outcomes. For instance, Solomon et al. (1992) conducted research in three elementary schools in an affluent suburban area in the late 1980s. They found that student sense of community was significantly correlated with the students' liking for school, empathy, prosocial motivation, academic motivation, and self-esteem.

More in depth research was conducted in 24 schools from six school districts by Battistich et al. (1995). Three of the districts were located in large cities, one was in a small city, and two were located in the suburbs of cities; three districts were on the west coast, one was in the south, one was in the southeast, and one was in the northeastern region of the United States. Approximately half of the students surveyed were Caucasian, 22% were African-American, and 21% were Hispanic. The researchers examined the effect of students' sense of community, as measured by the interpersonal relations in the school and the student influence on rules and decisions made in the school, on several student outcomes, including academic attitudes, social attitudes and behaviors, and academic performance (Battistich et al., 1995). The data are limited in that they come from a relatively small sample and are cross-sectional.

Within schools, Battistich et al (1995) found that student sense of community was significantly related to academic attitudes and social attitudes and behaviors. Similar results were found at the between-school level. Battistich et al. (1995) found that students' academic attitudes were significantly associated with sense of community, as were social attitudes and behaviors, such as conflict resolution, prosocial motivation, and altruistic behavior. Basic academic comprehension was also related to school community, although no other measure of academic performance was. Therefore, it seems that student sense of community is related to both academic and social attitudes, as well as social behaviors, but not to academic achievement. These findings support the idea that students in a communal school will feel more attached to the school and will exhibit more prosocial behavior that aligns with the values and norms shared by the school's members.

Battistich and Hom (1997) specifically examined the relationship between student sense of community and deviant behavior. Using the same data as the above study (Battistich et al., 1995), they found that levels of student sense of community were negatively associated with levels of drug use and delinquency. That is, schools with higher levels of student sense of community had lower levels of student drug use and delinquency.

Battistich and his colleagues have also examined the effects of communal school organization on teacher outcomes. Battistich et al. (1997) examined the relationship between teacher sense of school and teacher attitudes and perceptions. They found that teacher sense of community was highly correlated with teacher efficacy, teacher work enjoyment, and teacher satisfaction. Teacher sense of community was also strongly associated with teacher perceptions of principal effectiveness, parental supportiveness, and positive relations between teachers and students.

The importance of communal school organization can also be seen in the work Battistich and his colleagues have done on their Child Development Program, an elementary school intervention that helps schools become caring communities (Battistich et al., 1996). This intervention helps school develop a sense of common purpose and commitment to shared norms and values. A key aspect of the program is to build stable, warm, and supportive relationships between and among teachers, administrators, and students (Battistich et al., 1996).

Using the same data as the above research (Battistich et al., 1995), the researchers examined the effects of the Child Development Program on student outcomes (Battistich et al., 1996). Comparing schools that received the program with comparison schools over time, they found a statistically significant decline in alcohol use in the treatment school and a statistically significant increase in alcohol use in the comparison school. Similar results were found for marijuana use, however the results were not statistically significant. The researchers also examined differences in outcomes between schools with high program implementation, moderate implementation, and low implementation. Not surprisingly, the best results were shown in schools with high implementation quality. These schools exhibited a decline in alcohol use, marijuana use, weapon carrying, vehicle theft, truancy, and violent threats (Battistich et al., 1996).

Conclusion

The above discussion suggests the importance of the social organization of a school in general and, more specifically, the importance of communal school organization. Research has shown that schools with are communally organized have more effective teachers who enjoy their job more and have better perceptions of the school in general. These schools also have students who are more bonded to the teachers and to the school's norms and who exhibit higher academic achievement and less deviant behavior. Communal schools are characterized by a shared system of values, a common agenda, high levels of teacher collegiality, and an extended teacher role. These features clearly have powerful consequences for both teachers and students.

Previous research does, however, have many flaws and gaps. For instance, many of the studies do not examine the process leading from communal school organization to beneficial student outcomes. That is, they do not examine the question of *why* students in communal schools exhibit higher levels of academic achievement or lower levels of problem behavioral. Although some researchers propose that communal school organization leads to greater student sense of belonging which then leads to more positive behavior, most do not specifically test the middle component but jump directly from the school organization to the behavioral outcome. In addition, much of the previous research does not directly examine the relationship between communal school organization and the specific outcome of student delinquency; only Battistich and Hom (1997) specifically examine this association. Similarly, none of the research examines the relationship between communal school organization and victimization.

Another weakness of some past studies, specifically the research conducted by Battistich and his colleagues, is the data used. The findings of Battistich et al. (1995, 1996, 1997) are based on data from only 24 schools, which, for school-level research, constitutes a very small sample. In addition, these data are cross-sectional, thereby leading to questions of temporal ordering. That is, it is very possible that the positive attitudes and behaviors of students result in a communal school, rather than the other way around as suggested by the researchers. Another problem is the lack of control variables in many of the studies. By not including other variables that may affect communal school organization or the studied outcomes, researchers do not control for the possibility of a spurious relationship between communal school organization and the outcomes. That is, alternative explanations for the link between communal school organization and the studied outcomes are not considered. Nor have researchers considered the possibility of interactions between communal school organization and moderating variables such as school size and racial heterogeneity. Finally, some studies examined sense of community and behavioral outcomes at the individual level; this is a problem because communal school organization is clearly a school-level characteristic.

This research will attempt to reduce most of these weaknesses. It will examine the extent to which student bonding mediates the effect of communal school organization on delinquency. In addition, although the data used in this research is correlational, the sample size is far larger than that used by Battistich and his colleagues and the data will be analyzed at the school-level rather than the individual-level. Finally, statistical controls will be applied for alternative explanations, such as school size and racial heterogeneity, and interactions between communal school organization and these variables will be examined.

STUDENT BONDING

After examining the research on communal school organization, it is clear that students with a high sense of school community appear to be more bonded to the school. They have greater attachment to the teachers, more commitment to the school, and have internalized the norms of the school to a greater degree. They feel as though they belong to the school, as though they are valued and accepted.

A natural progression in discussions about student sense of belonging is to Hirschi's social control theory, as discussed in his book (Hirschi, 1969). Social control theory holds the assumption that humans are naturally deviant and must be controlled in order to prevent their involvement in delinquency. Delinquency, therefore, is the result of something missing, of the absence of a controlling force. This controlling force in Hirschi's theory is the social bond, the link between individuals and society, which restrains people from crime because they value the bond and do not want to damage it. Hirschi's control theory assumes that when a person's bond to society is weakened or broken, that person is much more likely to engage in delinquency. According to Hirschi (1969), the bond has four elements: attachment, commitment, involvement, and belief. Attachment is the affective and emotional element of the bond, the value individuals place on their relationships with significant others like parents, school, and peers. If an individual is strongly attached to someone, he cares what that person thinks of him and will, therefore, not want to do anything to disappoint that person. Therefore, an individual with strong attachment will be less likely to engage in delinquent behavior. Commitment is the rational element of the social bond, the value individuals place on the time, energy, and effort they have devoted to certain activities or institutions. If an individual is strongly committed to something, she will not want to engage in anything that might cause her to lose that investment. Therefore, an individual with strong commitment will be less likely to risk losing an investment by engaging in delinquent behavior. Involvement is the time spent in conventional activities. If an individual is involved in many activities, he simply does not have time to engage in delinquent behavior. Finally, belief is the extent to which an individual recognizes the legitimacy of societal norms and laws. If a person believes in the norms of society, she is more likely to behave in accordance with those norms. Therefore, an individual with strong belief will be less likely to engage in delinquent behavior. An individual's social bond is comprised of these four elements.

One domain in which an individual's social bond is formed is school. Hirschi discussed each element of the bond as it is exhibited in the school domain (Hirschi, 1969). Attachment to school is shown by the extent to which students care about the school and the teachers and the extent to which they care about the teachers' opinions. If students care very little about school and the teachers' opinions, they feel no emotional attachment to the school, and therefore deny the legitimacy of the norms and rules of the school. In other words, students who do not like school or the teachers will probably think that the adults in the school have no right to control them. These students are, therefore, much more likely to be delinquent. Commitment to education is shown by the time and energy students invest in school as they pursues the goal of academic achievement. Students who invest a lot in school and their education are more likely to be concerned about losing their investments if they are deviant. Conversely, students who invest little in school and their education will not have anything to lose, and are, therefore, more likely to be delinquent. Involvement is simply the time spent on conventional school activities. Students who spend a lot of time involved in school activities will have little time to become involved in delinquency. Finally, belief is the extent to which students give legitimacy to the norms and rules of the school. The less students believe in school rules, the more likely they are to break them. Essentially, students who are well integrated in school are less likely to be deviant. Those who have more positive associations, who have invested greater effort into school, who are involved in more school activities, and who believe in the rules of the school are less likely to engage in deviant activities (Welsh, Greene, and Jenkins, 1999).

Hirschi (1969) tested his theory on a sample of junior and senior high school students in the San Francisco-Oakland metropolitan area. The final sample consisted of 1479 black males and 2126 non-black males. The data consisted of school records, student questionnaires, and police data. Hirschi's (1969) findings provide support for his theory in the school domain. Students who cared little about what the teachers think and who did not like school, those with low school attachment, were much more likely to report delinquent acts. Additionally, those with low belief, who rejected the norms and rules of the school, and those with low commitment, who had low educational aspirations and expectations, were more likely to be delinquent (Hirschi, 1969).

Other researchers have supported the negative relationship between school bonding and delinquency as well (Krohn and Massey, 1980; Liska and Reed, 1985; Agnew, 1985; Thornberry, Lizotte, Krohn, Farnworth, and Jang, 1991; Cernkovich and Giordano, 1992; Jenkins, 1997; Welsh et al., 1999; D. Gottfredson et al., 2002). For instance, using self-report data from students in grades seven and twelve, Krohn and Massey (1980) found that school bonding explained some of the variance in the students' use of alcohol and drugs and engagement in delinquency. These findings were supported by Cernkovich and Giordano (1992). Using self-report data from students between the ages of 12 and 19, they found that the relationship between student bonding and delinquency existed for both Caucasians and African-Americans (Cernkovich and Giordano, 1992).

Jenkins (1997) studied school bonding in a sample of 754 middle school students in the seventh and eighth grades. She examined the effect of attachment to school, school commitment, school involvement, and belief in school rules on school crime, school misbehavior, and attendance. Commitment and belief were significantly negatively related to school crime, though attachment and involvement showed no effect. Attachment, commitment, and belief strongly predicted student misbehavior and nonattendance.

Finally, Welsh et al. (1999) examined student bonding in eleven middle schools in Philadelphia. Commitment to school, as measured by the amount of care and effort on school work put forth by the student, exhibited a strong negative relationship with student misbehavior. Attachment and belief were also significant predictors of student misbehavior.

Some researchers have criticized many of the above studies because they rely on cross-sectional data, thereby providing no information on the causal order between student bonding and delinquent behavior. These researchers discuss the possibility that the relationship between student bonding and delinquency is due to delinquency's effect on student bonding, rather than the reverse suggested by Hirschi (1969). In response to this criticism, some researchers have utilized longitudinal data to study the casual ordering of the relationship between bonding to school and delinquent behavior.

For instance, Liska and Reed (1985) studied the first two waves of the Youth in Transition data. The first wave of data were collected during the fall of 1966, when the subjects had just begun tenth grade, and the second wave was collected during the spring of 1967 as the subjects were finishing 11th grade. Examining the relationship between school attachment, parental attachment, and self-reported violence and theft, the researchers found the variables to be related in a causal loop. That is, parental attachment affected delinquency, while delinquency affected school attachment, and school attachment affected parental attachment (Liska and Reed, 1985). While a direct relationship was not found, school attachment and delinquency were indirectly related. That is, an increase in school attachment would result in an increase in parental attachment, which would then result in a decrease in delinquency.

Using the same data, Agnew (1985) examined the relationship between school bonding and delinquency. After conducting a cross-sectional regression of delinquency on student bonding at time one, he found that attachment had a significant effect on delinquency. However, when he conducted a longitudinal regression, the effects were much smaller. There was, however, a significant effect of time one delinquency on time two attachment, suggesting that the causal order between student bonding and delinquent behavior is the opposite of that predicted by Hirschi (1969). Agnew (1985) provided a caution with his findings by explaining that the majority of the variance for delinquency at time two was actually explained by delinquency at time one, thereby leaving little of the variance to be explained by student bonding at time one.

Thornberry et al. (1991) found results similar to Liska and Reed (1985) in his research. Examining three waves of data on 867 students in the seventh and eighth grades in Rochester, NY, Thornberry et al. (1991) found that commitment to school and self-reported delinquency were significantly related in a reciprocal loop. That is, commitment to school at time one was a significant predictor of delinquency at time two, while delinquency at time one was significantly related to student bonding at time two.

While more complex than Hirschi's original theory, these above findings from longitudinal studies still support the original hypotheses about school bonding and delinquency. It is important to note, however, that the effect of student bonding on delinquency tends to be smaller in longitudinal studies.

Little research has examined the relationship between student bonding levels and levels of victimization. However, G. Gottfredson and D. Gottfredson (1985) did find that schools with higher levels of student attachment to school and student belief in conventional rules experienced lower levels of teacher and student victimization.

More importantly for the current study, G. Gottfredson and D. Gottfredson (1985) highlight the importance of student bonding at the *school* level. All analyses in their study were conducted at the organizational-level, and the researchers concluded that schools with higher mean levels of student bonding did, in fact, have lower levels of school disorder. Since the current study focuses on rates of delinquency and victimization and levels of student boding at the school-level, this conclusion is particularly important.

The importance of student bonding can also be seen in the field of school-based delinquency prevention. Many programs focus on increasing a child's attachment and commitment to the school and to education. Social control theory suggests that deviant behavior can be prevented by increasing a student's bond, by giving the child something to gain if he conforms and something to lose if he deviates (G. Gottfredson, 1981).

An example of a school-based intervention that relied on social control theory was the Milwood Alternative Education Project (Elrod and Friday, 1986; Friday and Elrod, 1983; Gottfredson and Cook, 1986). This organizational-level project focused on increasing school levels of prosocial attachments, commitment to education, conventional involvements, and belief in the legitimacy of school rules. Interventions were created in order to better integrate students into the school. Although the project experienced some implementation problems, school-level measures of prosocial attachments, respect for the law, and social integration suggested that students were more bonded to the school. Greater support for the project is found in the outcome data, which show a significant improvement over the three year project: school averages of delinquency, drug use, and suspensions all declined while school attendance rose (D. Gottfredson and Cook, 1986). The results of this project also provide further support for the importance of student bonding at the school level.

A recent meta-analysis provided more support for prevention programs that focus on the relationship between student bonding and delinquency (Najaka, D. , and Wilson, 2001). Najaka et al. (2001) found that programs which resulted in increases in attachment and commitment to school also resulted in decreases in deviant behavior. They discussed several of these programs shown to increase student bonding. For instance, research on PATHE (Positive Action Through Holistic Education), another organizational-level intervention, has shown that the program improved student bonding, and thereby reduced deviance (D. Gottfredson, 1986). This program focused on building a school's capacity to manage itself through the use of teams composed of teachers, administrators, and students, who worked to improve the overall school climate and the academic performance of all students. The program also included services which focused directly on high-risk students. D. Gottfredson (1986) found that schools that participated in PATHE had higher school-level means of student bonding and lower school-level means of delinquency.

Conclusion

It is clear that student bonding is an important concept when discussing student achievement and delinquency. Research has demonstrated that students who are more attached to teachers, more committed to school, and have stronger belief in the school's norms will display higher academic achievement and less deviant behavior. In further support of this, it has also been shown that school-based prevention programs which focus on increasing students' bonds to the school are more effective at reducing problem behavior and increasing achievement.

This study contributes to the body of research regarding social bonding to schools in several ways. It will utilize a sample of 307 schools, far larger than other recent tests of the theory (Jenkins, 1997; Welsh et al., 1999). More importantly, it will examine a possible cause of student bonding, communal school organization, and analyze the relationship between these two concepts and the outcome variables of delinquency and victimization.

THE LINKS

Discussions about communal school organization naturally lead to discussions about student bonding. Research has demonstrated that students in communally organized schools have greater sense of belonging, greater commitment to the school, and greater internalization of school norms (Solomon et al., 1992; Battistich et al., 1995). As the adults in the school create a school community, the climate of the school becomes warmer and more inclusive. The students' feelings of belonging then increase, as do their levels of commitment to school and their levels of acceptance of school norms and values. These findings directly relate to Hirschi's social bonding theory. Student sense of belonging is equivalent to Hirschi's attachment, internalization of school norms is equivalent to Hirschi's belief, and student commitment to school is clearly the same in both sets of research. Thus, the link between communal school organization and student bonding is clear: students in schools that are communally organized will be more bonded to the school, as demonstrated by higher levels of attachment, commitment, and belief.

Organizational-level support for this link can be seen in LaFree's (1998) discussion of the legitimacy of social institutions. Institutions which have more legitimacy are those which experience greater ease in getting their members to adhere to institutional rules and norms (LaFree, 1998). These legitimate institutions then exhibit greater informal social control over their members (LaFree, 1998). This is clearly relevant to the school-level analyses conducted in this study. Communal schools with more supportive relations, common norms and goals, and high collaboration and involvement, would clearly demonstrate greater legitimacy to the students. These schools would therefore have greater informal social control over the students, as illustrated by higher levels of student bonding. This legitimacy would most clearly be seen in higher levels of the belief component of the student bond.

It is important to note the difference between communal school organization and student bonding, as they could be seen as the same concept on the surface. The major difference, however, is found in where each theoretical concept lies in relation to the individual. Communal school organization refers to the existence of a specific social organization that is external to the individual; that is, the existence of supportive relations, of collaboration, and of a set of shared norms and goals. Student bonding, however, refers to the internal processes that result from the existence of this communal organization in the school: the attachment to the school, the commitment to education, and the belief in school rules. Therefore, communal school organization is external to the individual, while student bonding is internal.

Continuing the progression, students who are more attached to school, more committed to school, and exhibit higher levels of belief in school rules and norms, are less likely to engage in delinquency (Hirschi, 1969). Similarly, schools with higher levels of student bonding are more likely experience lower levels of victimization (G. Gottfredson and D. Gottfredson, 1985). Therefore, it is expected that communal schools will higher levels of student bonding and lower levels of school disorder.

INTERACTIONS

Previous research has demonstrated that school size and racial heterogeneity hamper the creation and sustenance of communal school organization (Bryk and Driscoll, 1988). That is, schools that are larger and more racially diverse are more likely to have lower levels of communal school organization. Based on this research, it is expected that school size and racial heterogeneity will negatively influence communal school organization. However, this study will investigate these relationships further. Because Bryk and Driscoll's (1989) findings suggest that larger schools have greater difficulty in creating and sustaining communal organization, it is anticipated that communal school organization in these larger schools will actually have a greater effect on school disorder. That is, once a large school achieves high levels of communal school organization, the effect of communal school organization on school disorder will be greater in these large schools than it would be in smaller schools. The same effect is anticipated with regards to racial heterogeneity. Previous findings suggest that schools with more diverse populations have greater difficulty in creating and sustaining communal school organization (Bryk and Driscoll, 1988). Therefore, it is anticipated that if racially diverse schools do in fact achieve high levels of communal school organization, the effect of communal school organization on school disorder will actually be stronger in these heterogeneous schools than in more homogeneous schools. It is predicted that the strength of communal school organization will actually buffer the adverse effects that school size and racial heterogeneity may have on school disorder. Although school size and racial heterogeneity can have negative effects on school disorder, communal school organization can counteract these negative effects by increasing the focus on the communal aspects of the school, thereby improving the social organization and level of disorder in the school.

HYPOTHESES EXAMINED

Based on the above research, the hypotheses of this research are as follows:

Hypothesis 1:   Schools with higher levels of communal school organization will have lower levels of school disorder.

Hypothesis 2:   Schools with higher levels of communal school organization will have higher levels of student bonding.

Hypothesis 3:   The effect of communal school organization on school disorder will be mediated by student bonding.

Hypothesis 4:   Communal school organization will interact
                                with school size and racial heterogeneity
                                such that the effect of communal school
                                organization on school disorder will be
                                greater in schools that are larger and more
                                racial diverse.

CHAPTER 3

Study Data and Measures

DATA

The data used for this research are from the National Study of
Delinquency Prevention in Schools (NSDPS; G. Gottfredson et al.,
2000). This dataset contains information from the nation's schools
regarding what types of intervention, activities, and strategies each
school has in place to prevent problem behavior or to increase school
safety, and how well these activities were implemented. G.
Gottfredson et al. (2000) used a commercial mailing list that includes
information from the National Center for Education Statistics in order
to obtain a nationally representative sample. The researchers started
with a sample of 1287 schools, which were randomly selected from the
nation's schools. The sample was stratified by location (urban,
suburban, rural) and school level (elementary, middle, high), with each
stratified cell containing 143 schools. For example, the sample
contains 143 elementary schools in an urban setting and 143 high
schools in a rural setting. G. Gottfredson et al. (2000) expected to
obtain a 70% survey response rate, which would have resulted in a final
sample of 900 schools, with 100 schools in each location-by-level cell.

Collection of the data included six steps: program classification
and five surveys. For the first step, information on all types of school-
based intervention models was collected and classified. The
researchers used this information to develop a comprehensive
classification system of prevention strategies that could be found in
schools. The final taxonomy included 24 categories, including 14

33

different types of discretionary prevention activities, such as behavior modification activities or activities that involve school planning.

Based on this original 24 category taxonomy, a survey was developed and sent to the principals of the sampled schools during the spring, summer, and early fall of 1997. This Phase One Principal Questionnaire, the second data collection step, asked principals to identify the strategies used in their school to prevent delinquency, drug use, and problem behavior, or those used to increase school safety and order. The principals were also asked to identify the individuals in the school who were responsible for each of these strategies, as well as to report on certain features of the school, on past program implementation, and on school staffing. Information about the Phase One Principal Questionnaire can be seen in Table 1. Of the original 1287 schools, responses were obtained from 848 schools, a response rate of 66.3%. This response rate ranged from 74.6% for rural

Table 1: Response Rate Details for Principal Questionnaires

Survey	N	Response Rate	School-Level Details
Phase One (spring, summer, fall 1997)	1287 requested 848 responded	66.3% Range: 59% (urban high) to 75% (rural elementary)	34.2% elem., 34.0% middle, 31.8% high 30.5% urban, 33.3% suburb, 36.2% rural
Phase Two (spring 1998)	848 requested 635 responded	74.9% Range: 67% (urban high) to 84% (rural middle)	34.4% elem., 35.0% middle, 30.6% high 30.6% urban, 31.3% suburb, 38.1% rural

Source: G. Gottfredson et al., 2000

elementary schools to 59.0% for urban high schools. A breakdown of the responding schools shows 34.2% elementary schools, 34.0% middle schools, and 31.8% high schools. In terms of location, 30.5% of the schools were located in urban settings, 33.3% in suburban settings, and 36.2% were in rural settings. The researchers experienced many difficulties during the collection of this survey. Approximately 9000 phone calls and multiple material replacements either by mail or fax were needed to obtain the responses (G. Gottfredson et al., 2000).

The researchers collaborated with WESTAT, a local research firm, for the collection of Phase Two data. The sample for Phase Two consisted of the 848 schools which responded to Phase One. Phase Two data collection included a second survey sent to the principals during the spring of 1998. This survey asked the principal questions about certain policies and practices in their school, the amount of crime in their school, architectural and other features about the school, as well as personal information such as their biographical history and leadership style. Information about Phase Two Principal Questionnaire can be seen in Table 1. Of the sample of 848 schools, responses were obtained from 635, a response rate of 74.9%. Again, a large variation in response rates was found, ranging from 84.2% for rural middle schools to 67.1% for urban high schools. Of the 635 responding schools, 34.2% were elementary schools, 34.0% were middle schools, and 31.8% were high schools. In terms of location, 30.5% of the schools were located in an urban setting, 33.3% in a suburban setting, and 36.2% in a rural setting.

A second survey conducted during Phase Two was the Student Questionnaire, collected during the spring of 1998. Data were collected only from secondary school students; that is, students in middle schools, junior high schools, or high schools. This survey included questions about student participation in school activities, student knowledge of school activities, student victimization and delinquency, and school climate. The researchers planned to survey a representative sample of 50 students per school, and actually surveyed a mean of 52 students per school. When a roster with student gender information was available, students were stratified by gender and then systematically sampled. If gender was not known, the students were stratified by grade level and sampled. More information about the Student Questionnaire can be seen in Table 2. Data were collected

Table 2: Response Rate Details for Phase Two Questionnaires

Survey	N	Respondent-level Details	School-level Details
Student Questionnaire (spring 1998)	16,014 students from 310 schools 55.6% of 558 secondary schools in sample	48.7% male, 51.3% female 64.5% white, 35.5% non-white	58.7% middle, 41.3% high 28.1% urban, 31.6% suburban, 40.3% rural
Teacher Questionnaire (spring 1998)	13,103 teachers from 403 schools 72.2% of 558 secondary schools in sample	94.7% full-time, 5.3% part-time 8.3% at school 1-9 years, 41.7% at school 10 or more years 5.7% male, 64.3% female 7.2% white, 12.8% non-white	54.8% middle, 45.2% high 30.5% urban, 30.8% suburban, 38.7% rural

Source: G. Gottfredson et al., 2000

from 16,014 students from 310 schools, 55.6% of the secondary schools in the Phase Two sample. Of the 16,014 students, 48.7% were male and 51.3% were female, and 64.5% of the respondents were white, while 35.5% were non-white. At the school-level, 58.7% of the responding schools were middle schools and 41.3% were high schools;

28.1% of the schools were located in an urban setting, 31.6% in a suburban setting, and 40.3% in a rural setting. The mean within-school response rate for the student surveys was 71.2%.

Phase Two also included a Teacher Questionnaire, collected during the spring of 1998. Again, data were collected only from secondary school teachers, and included information on teacher participation in school activities, teacher victimization, and school climate. The researchers intended to survey every teacher in participating schools. More information about the Teacher Questionnaire can be seen in Table 2. Data were collected from 13,103 teachers from 403 schools, 72.2% of the secondary schools in the Phase Two sample. Of the 13,103 teachers, 41.7% had worked at the school for 10 or more years, while 58.3% had worked there for less than 10 years. In addition, 94.7% of the teachers worked full-time at the school. In terms of demographics, 35.7% of the teachers were male and 64.3% were female, while 87.2% were white and 12.8% were non-white. At the school-level, 54.8% of the responding schools were middle schools and 45.2% were high schools; 30.5% were located in an urban setting, 30.8% were in a suburban setting, and 38.7% were in a rural setting. The mean within-school response rate for the teacher surveys was 71.1%.

The NSDPS reported on teacher victimization rates, as well as student delinquency and victimization rates, based on the teacher and student questionnaires (G. Gottfredson et al., 2000). Teacher victimization was higher in middle or junior high schools and in schools in urban locations. Similarly, student delinquency and victimization rates were higher in middle or junior high schools than in high schools. When similar national studies of school crime are examined, these results are comparable (G. Gottfredson et al., 2000). The Fast Response Survey System (Heaviside, Rowand, Williams, and Farris, 1998) and the Safe School Study (National Institute of Education, 1978) also found more crime and delinquency in middle schools and in schools in urban locations. Another survey, the School Crime Supplement to the National Crime Victimization Survey, is slightly different in that it samples students through households rather than schools. This survey does provide similar results, however: younger students were more likely to avoid certain places at school, as were students in urban areas (Chandler, Chapman, Rand, and Taylor,

1998). Although the rates estimated in each survey differ in value, the similarity in patterns indicates the validity of the NSDPS as a measure of national school crime and victimization.

An analysis of the possible self-selection bias at the school-level using the Inverse Mills Ratio was planned. Self-selection bias refers to the possibility that the schools which did not respond are different in some way from the schools which did respond. This analysis would have examined whether this bias was significantly related to the outcomes of interest, delinquency and victimization. The Inverse Mills Ratio requires data from both responding and non-responding schools on variables possibly related to this response decision but not related to the outcomes of interest. However, the only variables with data from both sets of schools are variables thought to related to delinquency, such as information on the location and level of the schools and census data about the surrounding community. Therefore, this analysis could not be conducted.

Although the self-selection analysis using the Inverse Mills Ratio could not be conducted, G. Gottfredson et al. (2000) did examine correlations between school and community characteristics and survey participation. The correlations from middle or junior high schools and senior high or vocational schools can been seen in Table 3.

Schools located in small towns or rural areas were significantly more likely to have participated in all surveys except the first principal survey. Middle schools were less likely to have participated in the first principal survey if they were located in communities with a larger proportion of African-Americans, with higher male unemployment rates, and with more households that received public assistance income. Middle schools were less likely to have participated in the teacher and student surveys if they were located in communities with more female-headed households with children, a greater proportion of urban population, and more households that received public assistance. Finally, middle schools were more likely to have participated in all surveys is they were located in communities with a higher proportion of owner-occupied housing.

High schools were less likely to have participated in all surveys if they were located in communities with a greater proportion of urban population. Interestingly, high schools were also less likely to have

Table 3a: Correlations of School/Community Characteristics with Participation in NSDPS in Middle Schools

School or Community Characteristic	PQ1	PQ2	TQ	SQ
% Free lunch, missing data	-.03	.02	.02	-.01
% Black students	-.10	-.09	-.07	-.10
% Hispanic students	-.04	-.08	-.08	-.07
Location[a]	.06	.10*	.11*	.12*
Percent population Black	-.12*	-.09	-.09	-.08
Proportion population with some college	.06	-.03	-.04	-.06
Proportion housing units owner occupied	.14**	.13**	.16**	.16**
Male unemployment	-.11*	-.04	-.06	-.04
Households with public assistance income	-.12*	-.08	-.10*	-.07
Proportion of population urban	-.08	-.08	-.09	-.11*
Female-headed household with children	-.09	-.09	-.11*	-.10*

Source: G. Gottfredson et al., 2000

[a]Location coded 1 = large central city, 2 = mid-size central city, 3 = urban fringe of large city, 4 = urban fringe of mid-size city, 5 = large town, 6 = small town, 7 = rural

*p<.05, **p<.01 ; PQ1 = Principal Questionnaire One, PQ2 = Principal Questionnaire Two, TQ = Teacher Questionnaire, SQ = Student Questionnaire

Table 3b: Correlations of School/Community Characteristics with Participation in NSDPS in High Schools

School or Community Characteristic	PQ1	PQ2	TQ	SQ
% Free lunch, missing data	.06	.13	.18*	.14
% Black students	-.12	-.03	.03	.04
% Hispanic students	.00	.01	.04	.01
Location[a]	.12*	.16**	.12*	.14**
% population Black	.02	.06	.07	.06
Proportion population with some college	-.10*	-.16**	-.14**	-.14**
Proportion housing units owner occupied	.06	.08	.04	.00
Male unemployment	.05	.06	.10*	.03
Households with public assistance income	.04	.08	.13**	.09
Proportion of population urban	-.12*	-.17**	-.15**	-.11*
Female-headed household with children	.01	.01	.04	.01

Source: G. Gottfredson et al., 2000

[a]Location coded 1 = large central city, 2 = mid-size central city, 3 = urban fringe of large city, 4 = urban fringe of mid-size city, 5 = large town, 6 = small town, 7 = rural

*p<.05, **p<.01 ; PQ1 = Principal Questionnaire One, PQ2 = Principal Questionnaire Two, TQ = Teacher Questionnaire, SQ = Student Questionnaire

participated in all surveys if they were located in communities with a higher proportion of college-educated population. Finally, high schools were more likely to have participated in the teacher survey if they were located in communities with higher male unemployment rates and with more households that received public assistance income.

In summary, middle schools in less socially organized areas, urban areas with high unemployment, more public assistance, more female-headed households, are less likely to have participated. High schools follow a similar pattern in terms of urban location, however these schools are actually more likely to have participated if they are located in areas with higher male unemployment and public assistance.

FINAL SAMPLE

The final sample used in this study consists of the 305 schools that have data from both teachers and students. The sample includes 124 high schools or vocational schools (40.7%) and 181 middle schools or junior high schools (59.3%). One hundred and sixteen of the schools are located in rural settings (38.0%), 96 in suburban settings (31.5%), and 93 in urban settings (30.5%). The number of teachers per school range from five to 220, with a mean of 46.3, and the number of students per school range from 17 to 2912, with a mean of 735.9. Responses from the principal surveys indicate that the school-level percentage of non-white students has a mean of 33.7%, while the school-level percentage of non-white teachers has a mean of 12.9%. In this final sample, a mean of 19.42% of the student body was sampled and a mean of 14.18% of the student body actually completed the survey, resulting in a mean within-school response rate of 74.8%. The whole faculty of each school was sampled and, in this final sample, a mean of 76.0% of the faculty responded.

Although the sample is intended to be representative of the nation's schools, non-response at the school level resulted in a biased sample. The following figures regarding the nation's schools are according to the National Center for Education Statistics (2001). The final sample for this research contains a higher percentage of middle and junior high schools than the nation (59.3% versus 48.7%) and a smaller percentage of high schools (38.1% versus 51.4%). In addition, the breakdown by location differs: 43.2% of the nation's schools are located in rural areas, 32.2% in suburban areas, and 24.6% in urban areas. This can be compared with the study sample location breakdown: 38.1% are in rural areas, 31.3% in suburban areas, and 30.6% in urban areas. The average number of students per school differs slightly (673.5 for the nation versus 688.4 for this sample), as does the percentage of non-white students (37.7% for the nation versus 33.7% for the sample).

Due to the difference between the nation's figures and those of this sample, the use of statistical weights was considered. Weights were created to adjust for the bias introduced by non-response and to take into account the stratified sample design (G. Gottfredson et al., 2000). One set of weights was created that accounts for selection probability. Other weights, created to account for school-level non-response, are based on predictors of the probability of participation, such as school size and grade level composition. Finally, within-school weights were created to adjust for sampling and non-response. The final weights used in the original research are the product of the three weights described above (G. Gottfredson et al., 2000).

This study, however, will not use weighted data for several reasons. First, correlations using both weighted and unweighted data were examined and similar results were found. When the differences between the weighted correlations and the unweighted correlations were examined, none of the differences were significantly different from zero. In fact, only 24 of the 152 differences were greater than .05 (15.8%). Additionally, for 86 of the differences, the value of the weighted correlation is larger; however, for 66 of the differences, the value of the unweighted correlation is larger. Both the lack of meaningful differences between the correlations and the variability in the pattern of the size of the correlations suggest that there is not a significant difference between the weighted and unweighted data. The second reason for not using weighted data is due to the need to use a resampling technique that estimates the standard errors by accounting for the complex sample design, such as the stratified jackknife method that was used in the original research (G. Gottfredson et al., 2000). Given the lack of significant difference between the weighted and unweighted data and the complexities that would be introduced if weighting was used, this study will not use weighted data.

MEASURES

This research will take the organizational perspective described by G. Gottfredson and D. Gottfredson (1985), in which schools are viewed as "meaningful entities – social organizations that have measurable features that distinguish them from other schools just as individual people have features that distinguish among them" (p. 14). Schools, not individuals, are the focus here, and the differences among schools' levels of bonding, delinquency, and victimization will be examined, rather than the differences among individuals. Accordingly, all theoretical constructs will be measured at the school level.

The measurement scales are based on scales developed and copyrighted by Gary Gottfredson (G. Gottfredson and Holland, 1997; G. Gottfredson, 1999; G. Gottfredson and D. Gottfredson, 1999; G. Gottfredson et al., 2000). Table 4 shows the original scales, their sources, and the scale names used in this study.

Communal School Organization

Based on the research by Bryk and his colleagues, as well as that by Battistich and Solomon and their colleagues, several components of Communal School Organization have been identified and operationalized. In this study, Communal School Organization is made up of three components: (1) supportive and collaborative relations, (2) shared goals, norms, and values, and (3) consensus on communal organization. All variables for these components were taken from the teacher surveys, following Bryk's lead of defining a school's level of communal organization from the teachers' point-of-view (Bryk and Driscoll, 1988). Higher levels on the components represent a more communally organized school. Details about the three components can be seen in Table 5.

The supportive and collaborative relations component is operationalized by a scale made up of five variables that highlight the level of collaboration between and among the faculty and administration, the level of support felt by teachers, and the teachers' views of the relations between teachers and administration, teachers and students, and among the faculty. This scale is based on a scale

Table 4: Original Scales and Sources for Scales used in Study

Study Scale	Original Scale	Source for Original Scale
Attachment	Attachment	What About You (G. Gottfredson and D. Gottfredson, 1999)
Commitment	Commitment	What About You (Form DC) (G. Gottfredson and D. Gottfredson, 1999); NSDPS (G. Gottfredson et al., 2000)
Belief	Belief	What About You (Form DC) (G. Gottfredson and D. Gottfredson, 1999); NSDPS (G. Gottfredson et al., 2000)
Supportive & Collaborative Relations	Morale	Effective School Battery (G. Gottfredson, 1999)
Common Goals & Norms	Organizational Focus	EIS Organizational Focus Questionnaire (G. Gottfredson and Holland, 1997)
Delinquency	Student Delinquent Behavior	What About You (G. Gottfredson and D. Gottfredson, 1999)
Student Victimization	Personal Victimization	What About You (Form DC) (G. Gottfredson and D. Gottfredson, 1999); NSDPS (G. Gottfredson et al., 2000)
Teacher Victimization	Personal Security	Effective School Battery (G. Gottfredson, 1999)

Table 5: Communal School Organization items (N = 305)

Supportive and Collaborative Relations Range = 0 to 5, Mean = 3.85, SD = .80, α = .97	Factor Loading
The administration is supportive of teachers	.93
Administrators and teachers collaborate	.91
There is little administrator-teacher tension in this school	.91
I feel my ideas are listened to and used in this school	.90
Teachers feel free to communicate with the principal	.87

Common Goals and Norms Range = 0 to 10, Mean = 7.50, SD = 1.48, α = .94	Factor Loading
My school has clear focus	.94
Rules and operating procedures are clear & explicit in school	.90
It is difficult to determine what is expected of a person in school	.89
People are confused about what objective they should go for	.89
In this school, people know what to do and when to do them	.89
People said it is difficult to decide what aims to work towards	.88
Rules and procedures are often ignored in this school	.88
This school clearly signals what performance is expected	.87
The goals of this school are clear	.87
Everyone understands what behavior will be rewarded	.86

Consensus on Community
Range = 0 to 39.69, Mean = 3.34, SD = 3.28
Reciprocal of average of standard deviations for all items above

used by the original researchers of the National Study of Delinquency Prevention in Schools (G. Gottfredson et al., 2000). This component is based on Battistich's ideas of the importance of teacher participation and involvement, as well as Bryk's idea of "ethos of caring", illustrated by high levels of teacher collegiality, and Battistich's concept of a caring and supportive environment (Bryk and Driscoll, 1988; Battistich et al., 1995). All variables in the scale are binary true/false questions, and include statements such as "The administration is supportive of teachers" and "Administrators and teachers collaborate". Responses to the questions were coded so that a "1" reflected high support and collaboration and a "0" reflected low support and collaboration. The teacher responses to these variables were averaged at the school-level and then added together to form the Supportive and Collaborative Relations index. This continuous index has a possible range of scores varying from zero to five, where "0" illustrates low levels of supportive and collaborative relations and "5" illustrates high levels of supportive and collaborative relations. This aggregate scale has a mean of 3.85, a standard deviation of .80, and a reliability of 0.97. When a factor analysis was conducted, the variables all load highly on the one factor, with the loadings ranging from 0.87 to 0.93. This one-factor solution accounts for 81.59% of the variance among the variables.

The second component of Communal School Organization, shared goals, norms, and values, is operationalized by a scale made up of ten variables highlighting the commonality of direction and expected behavior in the school. This scale is based on a scale used by the original researchers of the National Study of Delinquency Prevention in Schools (G. Gottfredson et al., 2000). This component is based on Bryk's ideas of shared values and common agendas, as well as Battistich and Solomon's idea of common norms and goals (Bryk and Driscoll, 1988; Battistich et al., 1995). As before, all variables in the scale are binary true/false questions, and include statements such as "The goals of this school are clear" and "The school clearly signals what performance is expected." Responses to the questions were coded so that a "1" reflected high commonality and a "0" reflected low commonality. The teacher responses to these variables were averaged at the school-level and then added together to form a Common Goals and Norms index. This index has a possible range of scores varying from zero to 10, where "0" represents low levels of common goals and norms and "10" represents high levels. This aggregate scale has a mean of 7.50, a standard deviation of 1.48, and a reliability of 0.94. When a factor analysis was conducted, the variables all load highly on the one factor, with the loadings ranging from 0.86 to 0.94. This one-factor solution accounts for 78.54% of the variance.

The final component of Communal School Organization is consensus on community. This component was operationalized by taking the reciprocal of the average of the school-level standard deviations for all 15 variables used in the above two components. The idea behind this component is that schools with high levels of communal school organization should have higher levels agreement on the above questions. That is, not only should a communally organized school demonstrate high school-level means for the Supportive and Collaborative Relations and Common Goals and Norms scales, but should also have smaller standard deviations for these indices, thereby showing a high level of agreement and consensus among the faculty. Higher values on the Consensus indicator illustrate higher levels of communal school organization and lower values illustrate lower levels. The mean for this component is 3.34, with a standard deviation of 3.28.

When a varimax factor analysis was conducted on all 15 items together, a two factor solution is produced (Table 6). The two factors closely resemble the first two indices described above (Supportive and Collaborative Relations and Common Norms and Goals). All items loaded on the scales to which they were assigned, although a few of the variables also demonstrated high loadings on the other scale. This is not a large problem for two reasons. First, those variables still had higher loadings on the scales to which they were assigned. Second, these high loadings on other scales support the idea of a single underlying construct, Communal School Organization, which will be estimated in the structural equation models.

The correlations among the three components of Communal School Organization can be seen in Table 7. The high correlations suggest that, although the scales are distinct components, they are indicators of a single underlying construct.

Table 6: Factor Analysis of all Communal School Organization Items
(N=305)

Items	Supportive & Collaborative Relations	Common Goals & Norms
The administration is supportive of teachers	.76	.53
Administrators and teachers collaborate	.66	.65
There is little administrator-teacher tension	.84	.38
I feel my ideas are listened to and used	.74	.49
Teachers feel free to communicate with the principal	.91	.20
My school has clear focus	.41	.84
Rules and operating procedures are clear and explicit	.33	.84
It is difficult to determine what is expected of a person	.35	.83
People are confused about objectives	.48	.75
Rules and procedures are often ignored in this school	.42	.77
It is difficult to decide what aims to work towards	.40	.78
Everyone understands what behavior will be rewarded	.43	.74
This school signals what performance is expected	.27	.84
The goals of this school are clear	.27	.84

Table 7: Correlations among the Components of Communal School
Organization (N=305)

	Supportive & Collaborative Relations	Common Goals & Norms	Consensus on Community
Supportive & Collaborative Relations	1.0		
Common Norms & Goals	.811**	1.0	
Consensus on Community	.382**	.440**	1.0

**p<.01

Student Bonding

The theoretical construct of Student Bonding was operationalized based
on the definitions and elements presented by Hirschi (1969). This
construct includes three components: (1) attachment, (2) belief, and (3)
commitment. All variables for these components were taken from the
student surveys. Although Hirschi identifies a fourth element of the
social bond, involvement, this component was not included in this
research for two reasons. First, several theorists have argued that
involvement, meaning the amount of actual time spent engaged in
conventional activities, can not be sufficiently separated from the
element of commitment (Kempf, 1993). Second, researchers have
consistently found a lack of support for involvement as a significant
element of the bond and predictor of delinquency (Kempf, 1993).
Therefore, this research will examine only three elements of the bond:
Attachment, belief, and commitment. Higher levels on each of these
components indicate higher levels of student bonding. Details about
each of these components can be seen in Table 8.

Table 8: Student Bonding items (N = 305)

Attachment Range = 0 to 8, Mean = 5.00, SD = .59, α = .86	Factor Loading
I like school	.80
I am usually happy when I am in school	.78
I care what teachers think about me	.75
Teachers here care about students	.73
I like the classes I am taking	.69
I enjoy the work I do in class	.68
I am learning the things I need to know	.66
Most of the time, I do not want to go to school	.63
Belief Range = 1 to 7, Mean = 5.57, SD = .45, α = .87	**Factor Loading**
It is OK to take advantage of a person who isn't careful	.80
I want to do the right thing whenever I can	.79
If you find someone's purse, it is OK to keep it	.79
Sometimes you have to be a bully to get respect	.79
I want to be a person of good character	.77
I have a duty to be a good citizen	.72
You have to break some rules if you want to be popular	.62

Table 8: Student Bonding items (N = 305) (continued)

Commitment Range = 0 to 7, Mean = 5.27, SD = .47, α = .87	Factor Loading
I am proud of my school work	.80
I turn my homework in on time	.79
I try to finish all of my homework	.78
My grades at school are good	.76
I try to do my best at school work	.74
I usually quit when my school work is too hard	.73
I am satisfied with the way I am doing in school	.66

Eight variables are included in the scale used to operationalize the attachment component of Student Bonding. This scale is based on a scale used by the original researchers of the National Study of Delinquency Prevention in Schools (G. Gottfredson et al., 2000). The variables in the scale highlight students' emotional bonds to teachers and the school in general, as well as students' feelings of belonging. All variables in the scale are binary true/false questions, and include statements such as "I care what teachers think about me" and "I am usually happy when I am at school." Responses to the questions were coded so that a "1" reflected high attachment and a "0" reflected low attachment. The student responses to these variables were averaged at the school-level and then added together to form an Attachment index. This continuous index has a possible range of scores varying from zero to eight, where "0" represents low attachment to school and "8" represents high attachment to school. This aggregate scale has a mean of 5.00, a standard deviation of 0.59, and a reliability of 0.86. When a factor analysis was conducted, the variables all load highly on one factor, with the loadings ranging from 0.63 to 0.80. This one-factor solution accounts for 51.62% of the variance among the variables.

The belief component of Student Bonding is operationalized by a scale made up of seven variables dealing with students' feelings about breaking rules and the legitimacy of norms. This scale is based on a scale used by the original researchers of the National Study of Delinquency Prevention in Schools (G. Gottfredson et al., 2000). All variables in the scale are binary true/false questions, and include statements such as "Sometimes you have to be a bully to get respect" and "It is okay to take advantage of a person." Responses to the questions were coded so that a "1" reflected high belief and a "0" reflected low belief. The student responses to these variables were averaged at the school-level and then added together to form a Belief index. This index has a possible range of scores varying from zero to seven, where "0" represents low belief in the legitimacy of rules and norms and "7" represents high belief. This aggregate scale has a mean of 5.57, a standard deviation of 0.45 and a reliability score of 0.87. When a factor analysis was conducted, the variables load highly on the one factor, with the loadings ranging from 0.62 to 0.80; the single factor solution accounts for 57.24% of the variance.

Finally, seven variables make up the scale used to operationalize the commitment component of Student Bonding. The variables in this scale question the students about the effort and value they place on their schoolwork, grades, and homework. This scale is based on a scale used by the original researchers of the National Study of Delinquency Prevention in Schools (G. Gottfredson et al., 2000). All variables in the scale are binary true/false questions, and include statements such as "I am proud of my school work" and "I usually quit when school work is too hard." Responses to the questions were coded so that a "1" reflected high commitment and a "0" reflected low commitment. The student responses to these variables were averaged at the school-level and then added together to form a Commitment index. This index has a possible range of scores varying from zero to seven, where "0" represents low commitment to school and education and "7" represents high commitment. This aggregate scale has a mean of 5.27, a standard deviation of 0.47, and a reliability of 0.87. When a factor analysis was conducted, the variables all load highly on the one factor, with the loadings ranging from 0.67 to 0.80; the single factor solution accounts for 56.55% of the variance.

Table 9: Factor Analysis of all Student Bonding Items (N=305)

Items	Attach	Belief	Commit
I like school	**.80**	.06	.14
I am usually happy when I am in school	**.70**	.21	.25
I care what teachers think about me	**.60**	.37	.29
Teachers here care about students	**.58**	.35	.24
I like the classes I am taking	**.65**	.23	.08
I enjoy the work I do in class	**.80**	-.18	.07
I am learning the things I need to know	**.63**	.08	.24
Most of time, I don't want to go to school	**.56**	.18	.13
It is OK to take advantage of a person	.00	**.83**	.06
I want to do the right thing whenever I can	.38	**.69**	.12
If you find a purse, it is OK to keep it	.04	**.76**	.30
Sometimes you have to be a bully	.00	**.79**	.24
I want to be a person of good character	.24	**.69**	.29
I have a duty to be a good citizen	.40	**.56**	.24
You have to break rules to be popular	.28	**.58**	-.02
I am proud of my school work	.36	.15	**.72**
I turn my homework in on time	.09	.48	**.66**
I try to finish all of my homework	.36	.41	**.55**
My grades at school are good	.12	.26	**.74**
I try to do my best at school work	.37	.37	**.52**
I usually quit when school work is hard	.19	.40	**.56**
I am satisfied with how I'm doing in school	.18	-.17	**.82**

Table 10: Correlations among the Components of Student Bonding
(N=305)

	Attachment	Belief	Commitment
Attachment	1.0		
Belief	.456**	1.0	
Commitment	.561**	.597**	1.0

**p<.01

When a varimax factor analysis was conducted on all 22 items together, a three factor solution is produced (Table 9). The three factors closely resemble the three indices described above (Attachment, Belief, and Commitment). All of the items load on the scales to which they were assigned, although a few of the variables also demonstrated high loadings on the other scale. As with Communal School Organization, this is not a large problem for two reasons. First, those variables still had higher loadings on the scales to which they were assigned. Second, these high loadings on other scales support the idea of a single underlying construct, Student Bonding, which will be estimated in the structural equation models.

The correlations among the components of Student Bonding can be seen in Table 10. The high correlations suggest that, although the scales are distinct components of Student Bonding, they are indicators of one underlying construct.

School Disorder

School disorder has three components: student delinquency, teacher victimization, and student victimization. Details about these components can be seen in Table 11.

Student delinquency is operationalized by a 13 item self-report scale from the student survey regarding participation in a variety of delinquent activities. This scale was created by the original researchers of the NSDPS (G. Gottfredson et al., 2000). All variables in the scale are binary true/false questions, and include questions such as "In the last 12 months, have you hit or threatened to hit other students?" and "In the last 12 months, have you stolen or tried to steal things worth less than $50?" Responses to these variables were averaged at the school-level and summed to form a Delinquency index. The index has a possible range from zero to 13, where "0" represents low delinquent involvement and "13" represents high delinquent involvement. This scale has a mean of 1.66, a standard deviation of 0.72, and a reliability of 0.93. When a factor analysis was conducted, the variables all load highly on one factor; the single factor solution accounts for 59.05% of the variance.

Teacher victimization is operationalized by an eight item scale regarding a variety of victimization experiences. This scale was created by the original researchers of the NSDPS (G. Gottfredson et al., 2000). All variables in the scale are binary true/false questions. The scale begins with the question "This year in school have any of the following happened to you personally in this school?", which is followed by a list of experiences such as "Damage to personal property worth more than $10.00" and "Was physically attacked and had to see a doctor." Responses to these variables were averaged at the school-level and summed to form a Teacher Victimization index. The index has a possible range from zero to eight, where "0" represents low teacher victimization and "8" represents high teacher victimization. This scale has a mean of 1.24, a standard deviation of 0.59, and a reliability of 0.81. When a factor analysis was conducted, the variables all load highly on one factor; the single factor solution accounts for 48.48% of the variance.

Student victimization is operationalized by a seven item scale regarding a variety of victimization experiences. This scale was created by the original researchers of the NSDPS (G. Gottfredson et al., 2000). All variables in the scale are binary true/false questions. The scale includes questions such as "This year in school, did anyone steal something worth $1 or more from your desk, locker, or other place at school?" and "At school this year, did anyone physically attack and hurt you?" Responses to these variables were averaged at the school-level and summed to form a Student Victimization index. The index

Table 11: School Disorder items (N = 305)

Delinquency (In the last 12 months, have you...) Range = 0 to 13, Mean = 1.66, SD = .72, α = .93	Factor Loading
Broken into a building or car to steal or just look around	.85
Belonged to a gang that engages in fighting, stealing, drugs	.84
Stolen or tried to steal something worth more than $50	.84
Carried a hidden weapon other than a pocket knife	.81
Used force to get money or things from a person	.80
Been involved in gang fights	.80
Taken a car for a ride/drive without owner's permission	.77
Hit or threatened to hit a teacher or adult at school	.77
Purposely damaged/destroyed property not belonging to you	.76
Purposely damaged or destroyed property belonging to school	.73
Stolen or tried to steal something at school	.72
Stolen or tried to steal something less than $50	.68
Hit or threatened to hit other students	.56

Table 11: School Disorder items (N = 305) (continued)

Teacher Victimization (This year in school has any of the following happened to you?) Range = 0 to 8, Mean = 1.24, SD = .59, α = .81	Factor Loading
Received obscene remarks or gestures from a student	.80
Was threatened in remarks by a student	.79
Theft of personal property worth more than $10	.76
Theft of personal property worth less than $10	.74
Damage to personal property worth more than $10	.73
Was physically attacked but not enough to see doctor	.70
Was physically attacked and had to see a doctor	.57
Had a weapon pulled on me	.38

Student Victimization (At school this year, did anyone…) Range = 0 to 7, Mean = 1.49, SD = .35, α = .74	Factor Loading
Take things worth $1 or more by force, weapons, or threats	.74
Threaten you with a beating	.71
Force you to hand over money or things worth less than $1	.70
Physically attack and hurt you	.67
Threaten you with a knife	.63
Steal something worth $1 or more	.62
Steal something worth less than $1	.51

has a possible range from zero to seven, where "0" represents low student victimization and "7" represents high student victimization. This scale has a mean of 1.49, a standard deviation of 0.35, and a reliability of 0.74. When a factor analysis was conducted, the variables all load highly on one factor; the single factor solution accounts for 43.34% of the variance.

When a varimax factor analysis was conducted on all 28 items together, a three factor solution is produced (Table 12). The three factors closely resemble the indices described above (Delinquency, Student Victimization, and Teacher Victimization).

Not surprisingly, urban schools experience more delinquency than rural and suburban schools, with means of 1.74, 1.64, and 1.60 respectively. The means for middle schools and high schools are close to equal, at 1.65 and 1.66. A larger difference is found when schools are separated by both location and level. Urban middle schools has the highest mean delinquency rate by far (1.77), followed by urban and suburban high schools (1.70 and 1.67, respectively). These differences, however, are not statistically significant.

As with delinquency, urban schools experience far more student and teacher victimization than rural or suburban schools. The difference between the mean scores on the teacher victimization scale for location is statistically significant. Middle and junior high schools have higher mean victimization scores than high schools: student victimization has a mean of 1.63 in middle schools and 1.28 in high schools, while teacher victimization has a mean of 1.31 in middle schools and 1.13 in high schools. Again, urban middle schools have the highest means (1.66 for student victimization, 1.60 for teacher victimization), followed by rural middle schools (1.65 for student victimization and 1.23 for teacher victimization). For both teacher and student victimization, the difference in means when the schools were categorized by location and level is statistically significant.

As is always the case with self-report data, a discussion on the validity of these self-reports is necessary (Huizinga and Elliot, 1986). The question regarding self-report validity is based on whether the respondents are telling the truth about their delinquency participation and their victimization experiences. Problems arise when respondents do not tell the truth, possibly due to forgetfulness, exaggeration, or concealment. For the most part, researchers have found that self-report measures are relatively valid, although Huizinga and Elliot (1986) concluded that this finding cannot be taken for granted. However, the majority of the examinations of the validity of self-report data have been conducted at the individual level. Because within-school individual variance is treated as error variance in this study (i.e.: school averages are used), these examinations are not particularly relevant.

It is necessary, therefore, to examine the school-level validity of these measures of school disorder. One way to check the validity of these self-reports is to examine the convergent validity of measures from different sources, by examining the correlations between student delinquency, teacher victimization, and student victimization. Since all three scales are attempting to measure the level of disorder in schools, these scales should be significantly correlated. An examination of the correlations shows that they are significantly correlated (Table 13). Delinquency and Student Victimization have a correlation of .384, Delinquency and Teacher Victimization have a correlation of .314, and Teacher and Student Victimization have a correlation of .261.

Examination of the correlations between these scales and other self-report scales regarding school disorder produce similar results (Table 14) (G. Gottfredson et al., 2000). Teacher reports of victimization are highly correlated with teacher reports of school safety (-.72) and classroom order (-.77). Teacher reports of victimization are also highly correlated with student reports of school safety (-.62). Student reports of victimization were correlated with student reports of school safety (-.51), teacher reports of cblassroom order (-.34), and teacher reports of school safety (-.16). Finally, student reports of delinquency are highly correlated with student reports of schools safety (-.44), teacher reports of classroom order (-.31), and teacher reports of school safety (-.28).

Other school-level studies have found similar patterns in the correlations among measures of school disorder, thereby providing more support for the validity of these self-report measures (G. Gottfredson and D. Gottfredson, 1986).

Table 12: Factor Analysis of all School Disorder Items (N=305)

Items	Delinquency	Teacher Victim.	Student Victim.
Broken into a building or car	**.86**	.01	.04
Belonged to a gang	**.83**	.19	.07
Stolen something worth more than $50	**.86**	.16	-.14
Carried a hidden weapon	**.82**	.15	.01
Used force to get things from a person	**.79**	.11	.12
Been involved in gang fights	**.75**	.30	.19
Taken car for ride without permission	**.78**	.05	-.05
Hit or threatened to hit adult at school	**.71**	.36	.09
Purposely damaged property	**.74**	-.09	.24
Purposely damaged school property	**.70**	.02	.19
Stolen something at school	**.71**	-.12	.15
Stolen something less than $50	**.67**	-.06	.14
Hit or threatened to hit other students	**.46**	.17	.50
Received obscene remarks or gestures	.21	**.74**	.22
Was threatened in remarks by student	.21	**.77**	.03
Theft of property worth more than $10	.13	**.74**	.00
Theft of property worth less than $10	.09	**.67**	.35
Damage to property more than $10	.04	**.71**	.07
Physically attacked but saw no doctor	.03	**.72**	.06

Table 12: Factor Analysis of all School Disorder Items (N=305)
(continued)

Items	Delinquency	Teacher Victim.	Student Victim.
Physically attacked and saw a doctor	.04	**.59**	-.04
Had a weapon pulled on me	-.07	**.41**	-.02
Taken money worth $1 by force	.41	.29	**.49**
Threatened you with a beating	.30	.05	**.67**
Forced to hand over less $1	.35	.16	**.47**
Physically attacked and hurt you	.11	.05	**.68**
Stolen something worth $1 or more	.01	.08	**.74**
Threatened you with a knife	.65	.12	**.26**
Stolen something worth less than $1	-.17	-.08	**.74**

Table 13: Correlations among the Components of School Disorder
(N=305)

	Delinquency	Student Victimization	Teacher Victimization
Delinquency	1.0		
Student Victimization	.384**	1.0	
Teacher Victimization	.318**	.272**	1.0

**p<.01

Table 14: Correlations among School Disorder Components and
other Measures of Disorder

	Teacher Victimization	Student Victimization	Delinquency
Teacher School Safety	-.72	-.16	-.28
Teacher Classroom Order	-.77	-.34	-.31
Student School Safety	-.62	-.51	-.44

Source: G. Gottfredson et al., 2000

Control Variables

Several control variables were included in this analysis. These include student enrollment, student/teacher ratio, student gender composition, student age, student racial heterogeneity, teacher racial heterogeneity, neighborhood crowding, and neighborhood poverty. Including these variables guards against the possibility that the relationships between communal school organization, student bonding, delinquency, and victimization are spurious due to other characteristics of the school or the surrounding neighborhood. Details about these variables can be seen in Table 15, and the correlations among these control variables can be seen in Table 16. Other control variables were considered, such as the number of school-based prevention programs and neighborhood residential mobility, however these variables did not display significant correlations with any of the variables of interest in this study.

Student enrollment is the number of students enrolled in the school, while student/teacher ratio is the number of students divided by the number of teachers in the school. It was expected that these two variables would display negative relationships with communal school organization and student bonding and positive relationships with school disorder. A larger student body would make the creation of a sense of

Table 15: Means, Standard Deviations, and Ranges for Control
Variables (N=305)

Control Variable	Range	Mean	Standard Deviation
Student enrollment	17 to 2912	737.67	477.53
Student/teacher ratio	2.83 to 54.86	15.99	5.38
Student racial heterogeneity	0 to 0.25	0.14	0.08
Teacher racial heterogeneity	0 to 0.25	0.08	0.08
Percentage male students	0 to 100	48.25	8.89
Student age	11.63 to 17.30	14.17	1.50
Neighborhood crowding	0.01 to 0.70	0.14	0.09
Neighborhood poverty	-1.31 to 5.74	-0.05	0.83

community more difficult by hampering the development of supportive relations between teachers and students and among the student body and by reducing the amount of opportunities for all students to engage in active participation. This would, in turn, reduce the level of student bonding by decreasing the students' attachment to teachers and their commitment to school, and increase the amount of delinquency and victimization. Support for this can be seen in Bryk and Driscoll's (1988) study, in which a negative association between school size and communal school organization was found.

School gender composition is the percentage of students who are male. This variable was expected to positively correlate with delinquency and victimization; that is, schools with higher percentages of male students are expected to have higher levels of school disorder. This expectation is based on multiple data sources that have found a relationship between gender and delinquency (Federal Bureau of Investigation, 2000; Johnston, O'Malley, and Bachman, 2002; Johnson, 1992).

Table 16: Correlations among Control Variables (N=305)

	1	2	3	4	5	6	7	8
1	1.0							
2	.33**	1.0						
3	.17**	.05	1.0					
4	.15**	.20**	.21**	1.0				
5	.05	.05	.00	-.07	1.0			
6	.09	.00	.03	.06	-.09	1.0		
7	.03	.06	-.02	.30**	-.04	.01	1.0	
8	.03	.07	-.02	.39**	.04	.12*	.15**	1.0

1 = Student enrollment, 2 = Student/teacher ratio, 3 = Student racial heterogeneity, 4 = Teacher racial heterogeneity, 5 = Percentage male students, 6 = Student age, 7 = Neighborhood crowding, 8 = Neighborhood poverty

**p<.01, *p<.05

There are many choices that must be made when conceptualizing the race of students and teachers within a school. The first is the choice between absolute racial composition (i.e.: percentages of each racial group within the schools) and racial heterogeneity (i.e.: the diversity of racial groups within the school). Because these two terms are highly correlated, they cannot both be included in the analyses. Therefore, for this study, race will be conceptualized as the racial heterogeneity of students and teachers, because the idea of heterogeneity is more consistent with the theoretical framework of this study. The idea of community naturally brings about images of homogeneity. Therefore, conceptualizing race as racial heterogeneity will allow the exploration of the possible tension between community and diversity.

Student and teacher racial heterogeneity is expected to be inversely related to communal school organization, based on findings by Bryk and Driscoll (1988). The operationalization of student and teacher racial heterogeneity partially follows the suggestions of Miethe and Meier (1994). Miethe and Meier (1994) calculated racial heterogeneity as the product of the percent of African-Americans and the percent non-African American. However, the racial distribution within the school, as well as the correlations between different racial percentages and the variables of interest to this study, suggest a slightly different conceptualization of racial heterogeneity.

The racial distribution of students and teachers can be seen in Table 17. The percentage of African-American students ranges from zero to 99.69%, with a mean of 14.64%. The percentage of Hispanic students ranges from zero to 98.11%, with a mean of 10.09%. Finally, the percentage of Caucasian students ranges from zero to 100%, with a mean of 68.76%. The percentage of African-American teachers ranges from zero to 90.60%, with a mean of 7.21%, while the percentage of Hispanic teachers ranges from zero to 93.60%, with a mean of 4.75%. Finally, the percentage of Caucasian teachers ranges from zero to 100%, with a mean of 85.95%. Given the greater school- level mean percentages for both Caucasian students and Caucasian teachers, it

Table 17: Racial Distribution of Student Body and Faculty (N = 305)

	Range	Mean	Standard Deviation
Percentage of black students	0 to 99.69	14.64	22.80
Percentage of Hispanic students	0 to 98.11	10.09	18.69
Percentage of white students	0 to 100	68.76	31.91
Percentage of black teachers	0 to 90.60	7.21	15.58
Percentage of Hispanic teachers	0 to 93.60	4.75	10.86
Percentage of white teachers	0 to 100	85.95	19.77

makes more sense to combine the African-American and Hispanic categories when calculating racial heterogeneity, rather than the Caucasian and Hispanic categories as suggested by the Miethe and Meier (1994) calculation.

Stronger support for this change can be seen when the correlations between this study's variables of interest and the various racial percentages of the student body are examined (Table 18). The percentage of African-American students and the percentage of Hispanic students display similar correlations with the variables of interest, while the percentage of Caucasian students shows a very different pattern. For example, Communal School Organization has a significant negative correlation with both the percentage of African-American students and the percentage of Hispanic students and a significant positive correlation with the percentage of Caucasian students. Similarly, Teacher Victimization has a significant positive correlation with the percentage of African-American students and the

Table 18: Correlations between Student Racial Percentages and Variables of Interest (N = 305)

	Communal School Organization	Student Bonding	Delin-quency	Student Victim-ization.	Teacher Victim-ization
Percent black students	-.227**	-.174**	.143*	-.009	.381**
Percent Hispanic students	-.165**	-.049	-.022	-.027	.224**
Percent white students	.250**	.201**	-.112	.009	-.399**

**p<.01, *p<.05

percentage of Hispanic students, but a significant negative correlation with the percentage of Caucasian students.

Given the similar patterns displayed by the percentages of non-Caucasian students in relation to the variables of interest in this study, it makes more sense to operationalize racial heterogeneity as the product of the percent of Caucasians and the percent non-Caucasians. This was done for both the student body and the faculty. Using this calculation, the highest possible value would be 0.25, which would occur in a school with 50% Caucasian students/teachers and 50% non-Caucasian students/teachers.

An alternative conceptualization of racial heterogeneity, that would separate African-Americans and Hispanics, was considered. This value is calculated as follows:

$$RH = 1 - (proportionWhite^2 * proportionAfrican-American^2 * proportionHispanic^2).$$

This value represents the probability that any two people randomly selected from the school would be of two different racial groups. This value was calculated for both students and teachers and all models and interactions were analyzed using both this conceptualization of racial heterogeneity and the conceptualization discussed above. Similar results were found, with the exception of the interaction between Communal School Organization and student racial heterogeneity, which was significant only when this alternative calculation was used for student racial heterogeneity. This interaction will be presented in Chapter 4. With the exception of this interaction, the racial heterogeneity of both teachers and students is calculated following the first conceptualization discussed.

Control variables related to the neighborhood surrounding the school were obtained from 1990 Census data. Simonsen (1998) conducted a factor analysis of 15 standardized census variables and provided a varimax rotated two-factor solution that explained 61.1% of the variance. The first factor, neighborhood poverty, includes the following census variables: welfare (the average household public assistance income), female headed household (the rate of single females with children under 18 to married couples with children under 18), median income (the proportion of households with income below

$27,499), poverty (rate of persons below the 1.24 poverty level to persons above), divorce rate (the rate of persons over 15 years who are married to those who are separated, divorced, or have a spouse absent), and male and female unemployment (proportion of unemployed males/females in the labor force). Neighborhood crowding is a single census variable calculated as the ratio of households with five or more people to other households. These two variables are considered indicators of neighborhood social disorganization (Simonsen, 1998) and are, therefore, expected to be negatively associated with communal school organization and student bonding. In other words, schools located in a socially disorganized neighborhood are less likely to have high levels of communal organization and student bonding. Similar results have been found with regard to neighborhood collective efficacy (Sampson, 1999). These variables are also expected to be positively associated with school disorder. In other words, schools located in a socially disorganized neighborhood are more likely to have high rates of delinquency and victimization. Again, similar results have been found with regard to neighborhood collective efficacy and crime rates (Sampson, 1999).

The zero-order correlation between each control variable and each variable of interest (communal school organization, student bonding, delinquency, student victimization, and teacher victimization) was first examined. Each variable of interest was then regressed on all control variables that were significantly correlated with that specific variable of interest. If the control variable retained a significant effect on the variable of interest in this model, the path from that control variable to that variable of interest was included in the structural equation models. Results of this process can be seen in Chapter 4.

PLANS FOR ANAYSIS

Structural Equation Modeling

LISREL (version 7.16; Joreskog and Sorbom, 1989) was used to analyze several structural equation models. Complete structural equation models contain random variables, which represent either latent variables or observed indicators, and structural parameters, which illustrate the links between these variables (Bollen, 1989). Structural equation models have two major components: the latent variable model and the measurement model. The latent variable model is made up of unobserved constructs that correspond to theoretical concepts. This part of the equation gives information about the relationships among the unobserved latent variables. The measurement model is made up of the latent constructs and the observed indicators intended to measure these constructs. This part of the model gives information about the links between each unobserved construct and the variables used to measure each construct (Bollen, 1989).

The benefit of structural equation modeling is clear. It allows researchers to examine both measurement issues and structural issues. That is, these models can assess measurement quality and examine relations among variables at the same time (Kelloway, 1998). As Kelloway (1998) states, structural equation modeling is "roughly analogous to doing confirmatory factor analysis and path analysis at the same time" (p. 2).

There are five basic steps involved in structural equation modeling: (1) model specification, (2) identification, (3) model estimation, (4) testing of fit, and (5) model respecification (Kelloway, 1998). The first step is to specify the model to be examined, the purpose of which is to explain the correlation among the variables included in the model. The central element of the structural equation model is the covariance matrix of the sample. LISREL attempts to minimize difference between the covariance matrix of the sample and the covariance matrix predicted by the model; this process will be discussed in more detail later in this section.

The second step, identification, asks whether or not a unique solution for the model can be obtained, which deals with the number of known and unknown parameters in the model. If the number of knowns and unknowns are equal, the model is just-identified, and there is only one correct solution which would perfectly reproduce the sample matrix. If there are more unknowns than knowns, the model is under-identified, and no unique solution can be found. If there are more knowns than unknowns, the model is over-identified, and there are several unique solutions. The best situation for researchers is to have an over-identified model (Kelloway, 1998). If a model is under-identified, no solution is possible. If the model is just-identified, it may seem as though there is the perfect solution; however, one must keep in mind the many possible errors that may exist, such as sampling and/or measurement error. Therefore, what may seem to be the only and correct solution may contain much error. If the model is over-identified, there are many possible solutions, and LISREL's task then becomes to select the predicted matrix that most closely matches the sample matrix. Researchers can make a model over-identified both by assigning directional parameters and by fixing some parameters to a predetermined value (Kelloway, 1998).

LISREL conducts the third and fourth steps, estimation and fit testing, by using a process of iterative estimation to select the best match for the sample matrix (Kelloway, 1998). LISREL guesses appropriate parameter values, calculates the covariance matrix that would result from this guess, then compares this matrix with the sample matrix to see how closely the two match. If they match well, the estimation halts. If they do not match well, LISREL changes its guess, calculates a new implied matrix, and compares this with the sample matrix. This process continues until some criterion of fit has been reached; that is, until the difference between the predicted covariance matrix and the sample covariance matrix has been minimized. This research will use the mathematical function of maximum likelihood as the fitting criterion, the default used by the LISREL program.

The final step in the structural equation modeling process is model respecification or modification, which has the goal of improving the fit of the model (Kelloway, 1998). Modifying the model can either mean deleting paths from the model or adding paths to the model. The major dangers in this process is that changes will be made that have no theoretical basis or that cannot be replicated in other samples. To minimize these dangers, modifications should have some basis in theory and should be tested on a second, non-related sample.

Model fit can be assessed in three different ways. Researchers can examine the absolute fit of a model; that is, they can see how well the model reproduces the covariance matrix of the sample. Researchers can examine the comparative fit of multiple models; that is, they can compare two or more models to see which model provides a better fit to the data. Finally, researchers can examine the parsimonious fit of a model, which is based on the idea that a better absolute fit can be achieved by estimating more parameters. However, researchers must consider whether the loss of degrees of freedom, by estimating additional parameters, is worth the increase in the absolute fit. This study examined the absolute fit of the structural equation models estimated, the comparative fit of several models, and the parsimonious fit of these models.

Models Examined

In all models, the composition of the theoretical constructs was examined. That is, this study examined whether the hypothesized observable indicators of the latent constructs are accurate measures of that construct. The theoretical rationale discussed in Chapter 2 and the correlations shown in Tables 7 and 10 in this chapter suggest that the components of Communal School Organization and Student Bonding are indeed indicators of these two underlying constructs. To test this possibility further, the size, significance, and direction of the paths leading from each latent construct to its respective observable indicators were examined. To define a scale for each latent variable, the path from Communal School Organization to Common Goals and Norms was set equal to one, as was the path from Student Bonding to Attachment. Accordingly, it was expected that the paths from Communal School Organization to Supportive and Collaborative Relations and Consensus on Community and the paths from Student Bonding to Belief and Commitment would be close to the value of one and positive in direction. These measurement models can be seen in Figure 1.

Additionally, the measurement model for the dependent variables was examined. That is, this study examined whether Delinquency, Student Victimization, and Teacher Victimization are true indicators of School Disorder. The correlations shown in Table 13 in this chapter suggest that Delinquency, Student Victimization, and Teacher Victimization are indicators of a common underlying construct. However, since these correlations are not as high as those shown in Tables 6 and 9, it is also possible that the School Disorder indicators each have a unique component as well. Therefore, as can be seen in Figure 1, the measurement model for School Disorder is more complicated than the previous two measurement models: The three indicators of the latent construct School Disorder were estimated as both latent variables and observed scales. This is to allow for the possibility of other variables affecting one indicator above and beyond the effect on the indicators' common underlying construct. Specifically, previous analyses (G. Gottfredson, D. Gottfredson, Payne, and N. Gottfredson, 2004) suggest that Communal School Organization might affect Teacher Victimization differently than Delinquency and Student Victimization. That is, Communal School Organization might have an effect on Teacher Victimization separately, beyond its effect on the latent construct that represents what the three dependent variables have in common. In order to examine this possibility, each dependent variable will be estimated as a separate latent construct, with a fourth latent construct representing the School Disorder factor.

Figure 1 depicts the model for Hypothesis 1, which was estimated to test the hypothesis that schools with higher levels of communal school organization have lower levels of school disorder. To test this hypothesis, the direction and significance of the path leading from the latent construct Communal School Organization to the latent construct School Disorder was examined. It was expected that this path would be significant and negative. In addition, the paths leading from the control variables to specific latent constructs were examined. The standardized residuals and modification indices were also examined to look for any patterns among the variables that suggest a lack of fit with the data.

Figure 2 depicts the model for Hypothesis 2, which was estimated to test the hypothesis that schools with higher levels of communal school organization have higher levels of student bonding. To test this hypothesis, the direction and significance of the path leading from the latent construct Communal School Organization to the latent construct Student Bonding was examined. It was expected that this path would be significant and positive. In addition, the paths leading from the control variables to both latent constructs were examined. Standardized residuals and modification indices were also examined to look for any patterns among the variables that suggest a lack of fit with the data.

Finally, Figure 3 depicts the model for Hypothesis 3, which was estimated to test the hypothesis that the effect of communal school organization on school disorder is mediated by student bonding. To test this hypothesis, the direction and significance of the paths from Communal School Organization to Student Bonding and School Disoerder and from Student Bonding to School Disorder were

Figure 1: Model Estimated for Hypothesis 1

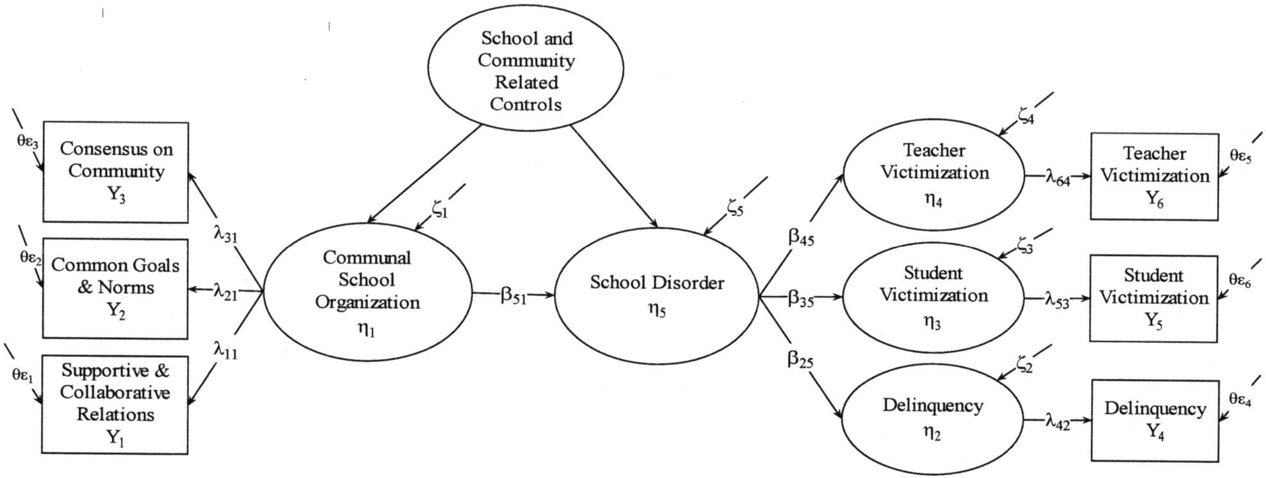

Figure 2: Model Estimated for Hypothesis 2

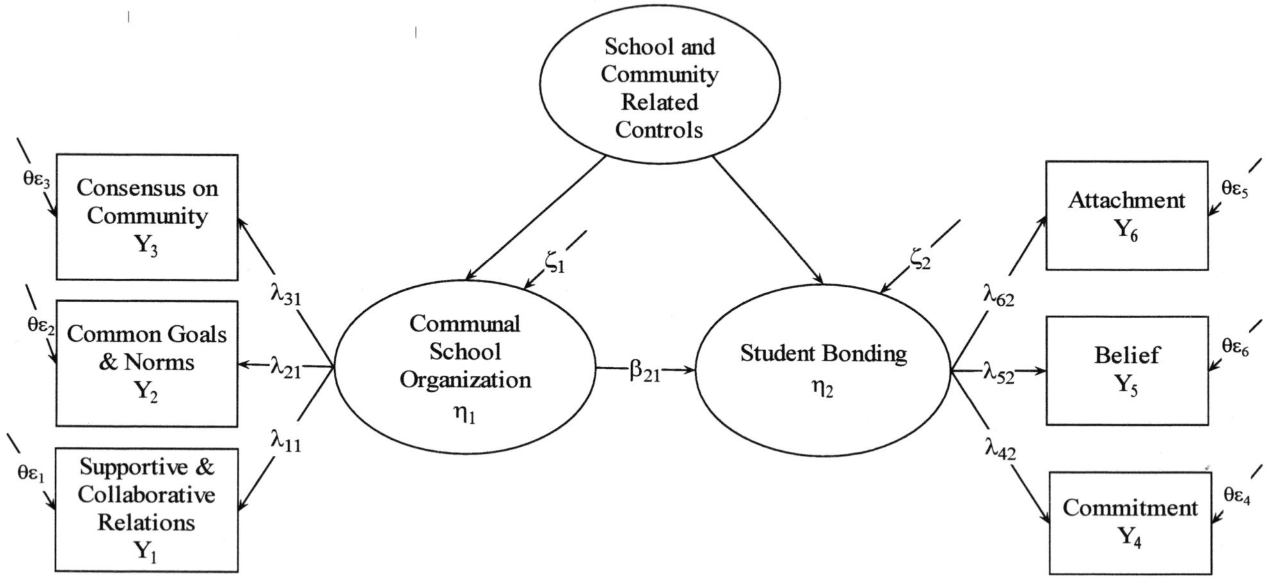

Figure 3: Model Estimated for Hypothesis 3

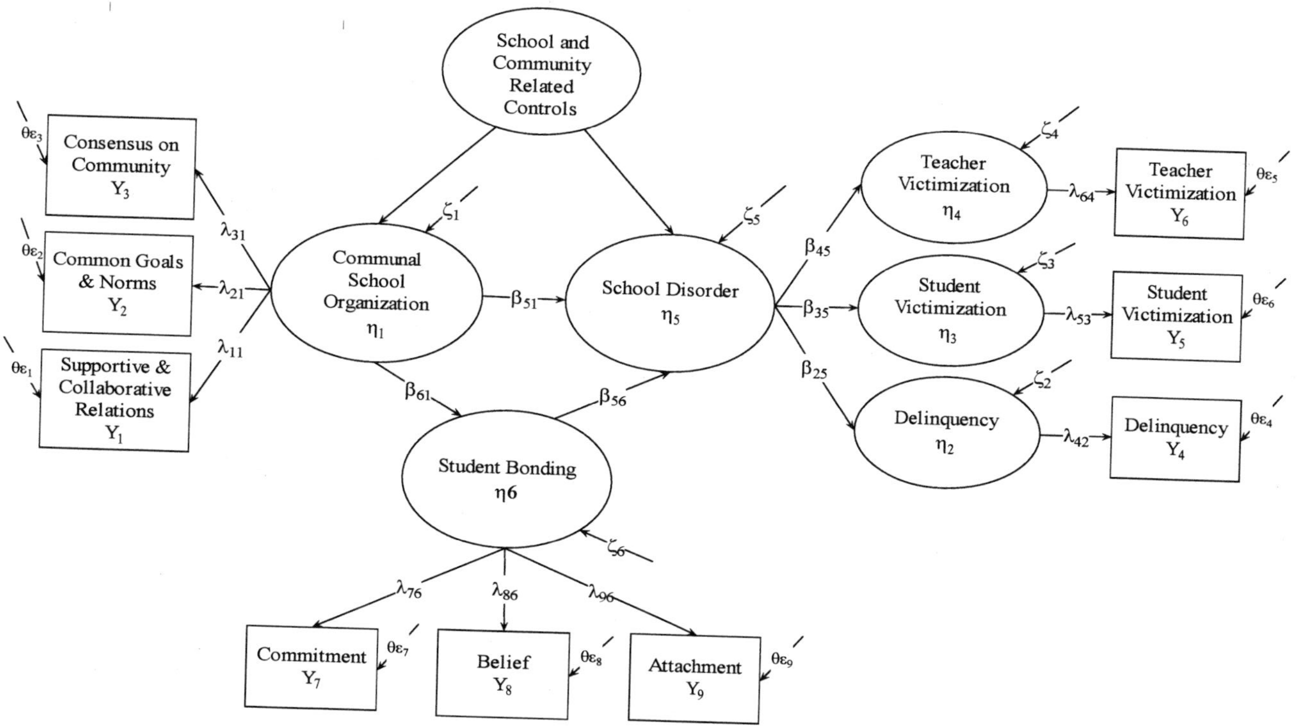

examined. It was expected that the path from Communal School Organization to Student Bonding would be significant and in a positive direction and that the path from Student Bonding to School Disorder would be significant and in a negative direction. It was also expected that the path from Communal School Organization to School Disorder would be either nonsignificant or smaller than the same path in Model One. As before, the paths leading from the control variables to latent constructs were also examined. The standardized residuals and modification indices were also examined to look for any patterns among the variables that suggest a lack of fit with the data.

Interactions

This study also investigated the potential moderating effect of school size and racial diversity; that is, the possibility that these factors interact with Communal School Organization to affect School Disorder. To examine this possibility, student enrollment, student/teacher ratio, student racial heterogeneity, and teacher racial heterogeneity were each multiplied by Communal School Organization. Student enrollment and student/teacher ratio were considered indicators of school size, while student racial heterogeneity and teacher racial heterogeneity were considered indicators of racial diversity. School Disorder was then regressed on these interaction terms to see if any term had a significant effect. Delinquency, Teacher Victimization, and Student Victimization were also regressed separately on the interaction terms to see if any had a significant effect on the individual indicators of school disorder.

To examine the effects of significant interactions terms, the sample was split at the 50th percentile point for one of the components of the interaction term (e.g.: larger versus smaller schools) and the outcome variable was regressed on the other component of the interaction term (e.g.: Communal School Organization) and control variables. This process was then conducted again, with the other component of the interaction term (e.g.: Communal School Organization) being split at the 50th percentile point. This process will be discussed in more detail in Chapter 4.

It was expected that the interactions between Communal School Organization and student enrollment, student/teacher ratio, student racial heterogeneity, and teacher racial heterogeneity would be significant. It was also expected that the effect of Communal School Organization on School Disorder and its indicators would be greater in schools that have larger student bodies, more students per teacher, and more racially diverse student and faculty populations.

CHAPTER 4

Relationships among Communal School Organization, Student Bonding, and School Disorder: Study Results

MEASUREMENT MODELS

This study first examined the measurement models of the latent variables Communal School Organization, Student Bonding, and School Disorder, in order to determine whether the observed scales are true indicators of their respective latent constructs.

As can be seen in Figure 4, the path from Communal School Organization to Common Norms and Goals was set equal to one. The values of the remaining paths in the measurement model display the expected directions and strengths. The path from Communal School Organization to Supportive and Collaborative Relations has a value of .868, while the path from Communal School Organization to Consensus on Community has a value of .471. Clearly, a large part of the variation of each of the observed indicators is driven by the latent construct Communal School Organization.

Figure 4: Measurement Model for Communal School Organization

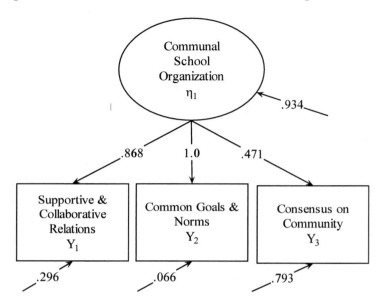

The measurement model for Student Bonding can be seen in Figure 5. The path from Student Bonding to Commitment was set equal to one. The remaining paths display values in the expected direction and strength. The path from Student Bonding to Attachment has a value of .764 and the path from Student Bonding to Commitment has a value of .813. Again, it is clear that a large part of the variation of each of the observed indicators is driven by the latent construct Student Bonding.

The measurement model for School Disorder can be seen in Figure 6. This measurement model is more complicated than the previous two models, as the three indicators of the latent construct School Disorder were estimated as both latent variables and observed scales. This is to allow for the possibility of other variables affecting one indicator above and beyond the effect on the indicators' common underlying construct.

Figure 5: Measurement Model for Student Bonding

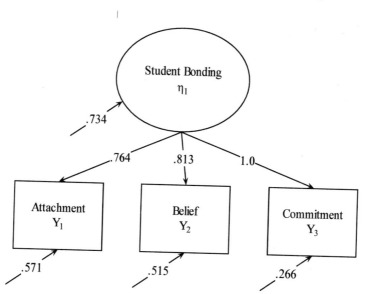

The paths from the latent constructs Delinquency, Student Victimization, and Teacher Victimization to their respective observed scales were set equal to the value of the square root of the reliability of each scale, with the error term equal to one minus the reliability value. The paths from School Disorder to each of the indicators were estimated as betas with the path from School Disorder to Delinquency set equal to one. The remaining paths display values in the expected direction and strength. The path from School Disorder to Student Victimization has a value of .962 and the path from School Disorder to Teacher Victimization has a value of .760. As with the other measurement models, it is clear that a large part of the variation of each of the observed indicators is driven by the latent construct School Disorder.

Figure 6: Measurement Model for School Disorder

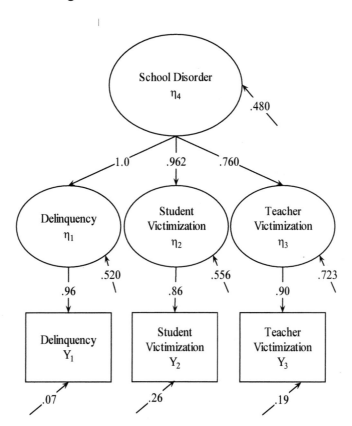

CONTROL VARIABLES

Following the process described in Chapter 3, the zero-order correlations of the control variables with the variables of interest were first examined (Table 19). Communal School Organization is negatively correlated with student enrollment (-.219, p<.01), teacher racial heterogeneity (-.266, p<.01), student age (-.126, p<.05), and neighborhood crowding (-.143, p<.05). This suggests that higher levels of communal school organization are more likely to occur in schools that have fewer and younger students and a less racially heterogenious faculty. Higher levels of communal school organization are also more likely to occur in schools that are located in less crowded neighborhoods.

Student Bonding is negatively correlated with student/teacher ratio (-.253, p<.01), student age (-.138, p<.05), teacher racial heterogeneity (-.117, p<.05), and percent male students (-.143, p<.05), indicating that higher levels of student bonding are more likely to occur in schools that have fewer students per teacher, younger students, a less racially heterogeneous faculty, and a smaller percentage of male students.

Finally, School Disorder is positively correlated with student/teacher ratio (.245, p<.01), student racial heterogeneity (.154, p<.05), teacher racial heterogeneity (.183, p<.01), percent male students (.151, p<.01), neighborhood crowding (.162, p<.01), and neighborhood poverty (.252, p<.01). Schools with more students per teachers, a more racially heterogeneous faculty and student body, and a greater percentage of male students are more likely to have higher levels of school disorder. Also, schools located in neighborhoods that have higher levels of residential crowding and poverty are more likely to have higher levels of school disorder.

Each variable of interest was then regressed on all control variables that were found to significantly correlate with that specific variable of interest (Table 20). This was done to ensure that the association between each control variable and variable of interest is not spurious, that the relationship still exists when other variables are included in the equation. If the control variable retained a significant effect on the variable of interest in the regression equation, the path from that control variable to the variable of interest was included in the structural equation models.

Table 19: Correlations of Control Variables with Variables of Interest
(N=305)

	Communal School Organization	Student Bonding	School Disorder
Student Enrollment	-.171**	.037(ns)	-.037(ns)
Student/Teacher Ratio	-.104(ns)	-.163**	.148*
Student Racial Heterogeneity	-.023(ns)	-.059(ns)	.155*
Teacher Racial Heterogeneity	-.263**	-.118*	.186**
Percentage Male Students	.043(ns)	-.157*	.163**
Student Age	-.113*	-.139*	-.096(ns)
Neighborhood Crowding	-.146*	-.094(ns)	.160**
Neighborhood Poverty	-.070(ns)	-.108(ns)	.251**

**p<.01, *p<.05

Based on this process, the following control variables were included in the structural equation models: Teacher racial heterogeneity and student enrollment were included as control variables on Communal School Organization, while percent male students and student/teacher ratio were included as control variables on Student Bonding. Finally, neighborhood poverty, percent male students,

Table Twenty: Standardized Regression Coefficients for Variables of Interest on Control Variables (N=305)

	Communal School Organization	Student Bonding	School Disorder
Student Enrollment	-.111*	---	---
Student/Teacher Ratio	---	-.143*	.090*
Student Racial Heterogeneity	---	---	.161*
Teacher Racial Heterogeneity	-.249**	-.060(ns)	.049(ns)
Percentage Male Students	---	-.166**	.157*
Student Age	-.083(ns)	-.088(ns)	---
Neighborhood Crowding	-.069(ns)	---	.118(ns)
Neighborhood Poverty	---	---	.147*

$**p<.01, *p<.05$

student racial heterogeneity, and student/teacher ratio were included as control variables on School Disorder.

HYPOTHESIS ONE

Hypothesis 1, as presented in Chapter 2, states that schools with higher levels of communal school organization will have lower levels of school disorder. The results for the structural equation model estimated for this hypothesis can be seen in Figure 7. This model has a Chi-Square value of 210.74 (66 degrees of freedom) and a Goodness-of-Fit Index of .903. The Chi-Square and the Goodness-of-Fit assess the absolute fit of the model to the data. The goal of the Chi-Square is to obtain a nonsignificant value; however, with large samples like this one, it is unlikely that one would achieve this goal (Kelloway, 1998). The Chi-Square is more valuable when comparing the fit of two different models, as will be done with the second estimation of Model One. The Goodness-of-Fit Index (GFI) ranges from zero to one, with a value around 0.9 indicating a good fit to the data; because this index has an unknown sampling distribution, this index is also more valuable when comparing the fit of two different models. The R-squared value for the School Disorder construct is .220, indicating that this model accounts for 22% of the variance of this construct.

In this model, the path leading from Communal School Organization to School Disorder was estimated. The expectation that this path would be significant and in the negative direction was confirmed: Communal School Organization has a significant negative effect on School Disorder (-.189, p<.01), indicating schools that are more communally organized have lower levels of school disorder.

Significant effects were also found with regards to the control variables. Communal School Organization is negatively affected by both teacher racial heterogeneity (-.235, p<.01) and student enrollment (-.159, p<.01). This suggests that schools with smaller student bodies and less racially heterogeneous faculty bodies have higher levels of communal school organization.

Student/teacher ratio has a significant positive effect on School Disorder (.157, p<.01), indicating that schools with larger student/teacher ratios have higher levels of school disorder. Percent male students also has a positive effect on School Disorder (.150, p<.01), suggesting that schools which have larger percentages of male students have higher levels of school disorder. Finally, student racial heterogeneity positively affects School Disorder (.126, p<.01),

Figure 7: Results for Model Estimated for Hypothesis 1 (First Estimation)

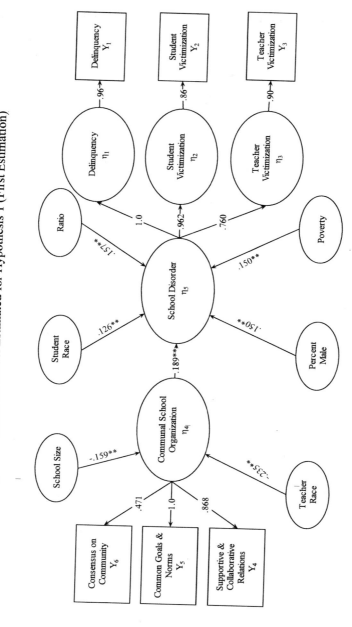

Figure 8: Results for Model Estimated for Hypothesis 1 (Second Estimation)

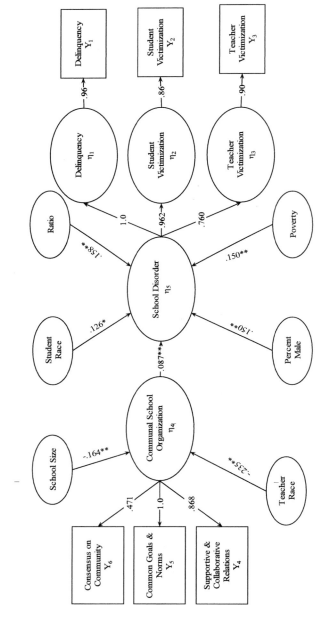

indicating that schools with more racially heterogeneous student bodies have higher levels of school disorder.

The control variable describing the community surrounding the school also displays a significant effect. Neighborhood poverty has a significant positive effect on School Disorder (.150, p<.01), indicating that schools located in poorer neighborhoods have higher rates of school disorder.

In this model, the modification index for the path from Communal School Organization to Teacher Victimization is 57.64, suggesting that this path should be freed. Therefore, Model 1 was estimated again with this path freed.

The results of the second estimation can be seen in Figure 8. All paths that were significant in the first estimation are still significant in the second estimation, with minor changes in some values. The path from Communal School Organization to School Disorder remains significant, although it does decrease in size (-.087, p<.05). The newly freed path from Communal School Organization to Teacher Victimization is significant and negative (-.496, p<.01), indicating that schools that are more communally organized have lower rates of teacher victimization. This also indicates that the negative effect of Communal School Organization on School Disorder found in the first estimation of Model One is largely due to the effect of Communal School Organization on Teacher Victimization. Thus, when the direct path from Communal School Organization to Teacher Victimization is freed, the path from Communal School Organization to School Disorder becomes smaller in size.

This new model has no modification indices or standardized residuals of interest. The model has a Chi-Square value of 153.71 (65 degrees of freedom), which is significantly less than the Chi-Square of the first model. This indicates that the model from the second estimation provides a significantly better fit to the data. The GFI for the second estimation is larger (.926), also indicating a better fit to the data. The R-squared value for School Disorder is slightly lower (.174); this is not unexpected, as a portion of the R-squared value in the first estimation is attributable to the effect of Communal School

Organization on Teacher Victimization, which was separately estimated in the second estimation.

The results of the estimation of Model 1 provide support for Hypothesis 1. Schools with higher levels of communal school organization do have lower levels of school disorder, as shown by the significant negative value of the path from Communal School Organization to School Disorder. Once a direct path from Communal School Organization to Teacher Victimization is estimated, the path from Communal School Organization to School Disorder becomes smaller, but remains significant and negative, thereby still supporting Hypothesis 1.

HYPOTHESIS TWO

Hypothesis 2, as presented in Chapter 2, states that schools with higher levels of communal school organization will have higher levels of student bonding. The results for the structural equation model estimated for this hypothesis can be seen in Figure 9. This model has a Chi-Square value of 96.81 (40 degrees of freedom). The GFI value is .941, indicating a good fit to the data. Finally, the R-squared value for the Student Bonding construct is .148, indicating that the model explains 14.8% of the variance of this construct.

In this model, a path from Communal School Organization to Student Bonding was estimated, with the expectation that this path would be significant and positive. This expectation was confirmed: Communal School Organization has a significant positive effect on Student Bonding (.205, $p<.01$). In other words, schools that are more communally organized do have higher levels of student bonding.

All control variables included in the model have significant effects. Student enrollment negatively influences Communal School Organization (-.119, $p<.01$), suggesting that larger schools are less communally organized. Teacher racial heterogeneity also negatively affects Communal School Organization (-.229, $p<.01$), indicating that schools with more diverse faculty bodies are less communally organized.

Figure 9: Results for Model Estimated for Hypothesis 2

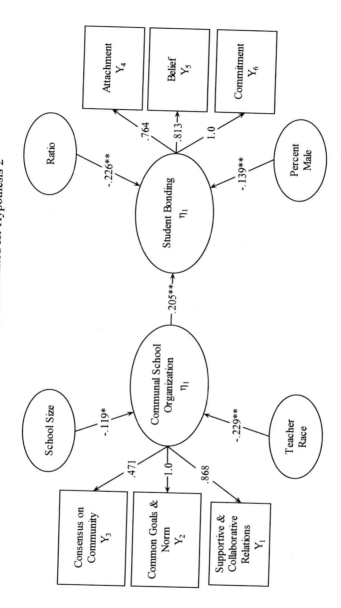

Figure 10: Results for Model Estimated for Hypothesis 3 (First Estimation)

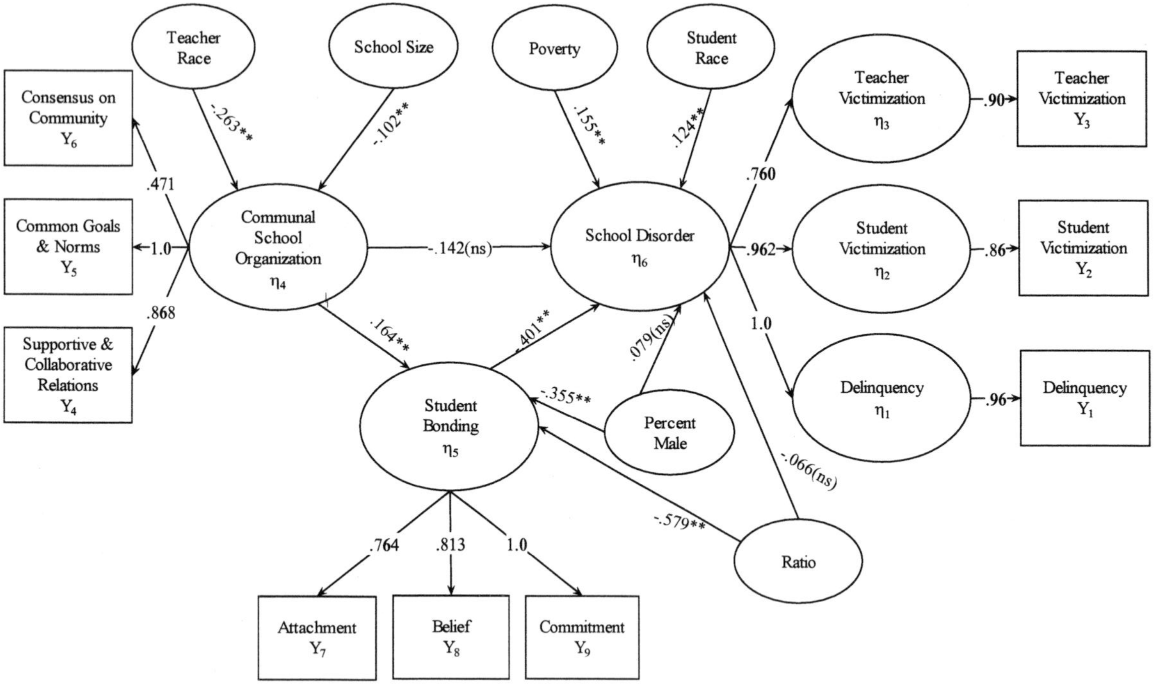

Student Bonding is negatively affected by percent male students (-.139, p<.01) and student/teacher ratio (-.226, p<.01), indicating that schools with a smaller percentage of male students and a smaller student/teacher ratio have higher levels of student bonding.

The results of the estimation of Model 2 provide support for Hypothesis 2. As shown by the significant positive value of the path from Communal School Organization to Student Bonding, schools with higher levels of communal school organization also have higher levels of student bonding.

HYPOTHESIS THREE

Hypothesis 3, as presented in Chapter 2, states that the effect of communal school organization on levels of school disorder will be mediated by levels of student bonding. The results for the structural equation model estimated for this hypothesis can be seen in Figure 10. This model has a Chi-Square value of 347.27 (95 degrees of freedom), and the GFI value is .872. The R-squared value for School Disorder is .423, indicating that 42.3% of the variance of this construct is explained by this model. This R-squared value is larger than the R-squared for School Disorder found in Model 1, suggesting that the inclusion of Student Bonding into the model increases the amount of variance of School Disorder explained by the model.

In this model, a path from Communal School Organization to Student Bonding was estimated, with the expectation that this path would be significant and positive. This expectation was confirmed. As in Model Two, Communal School Organization has a significant positive effect on Student Bonding (.164, p<.01). This confirms that more communally organized schools have higher levels of student bonding.

A path was also estimated from Student Bonding to School Disorder. The expectation that this path would be significant and in the negative direction was confirmed. Student Bonding has a significant and strong negative effect on School Disorder (-.401, p<.01), indicating that schools with higher levels of student bonding have lower levels school disorder.

Finally, a path was estimated from Communal School Organization to School Disorder, with the expectation that this path would either be nonsignificant or significant and negative but smaller than the same path in Model 1, due to the inclusion of Student Bonding in Model Three. This expectation was confirmed. Communal School Organization has a nonsignificant direct effect on School Disorder, indicating that the negative effect of Communal School Organization on School Disorder seen in Model One is mediated through Student Bonding as hypothesized.

Significant effects were also found with regards to the control variables. As in the previous models, Communal School Organization is negatively affected by both teacher racial heterogeneity (-.263, p<.01) and student enrollment (-.102, p<.01), indicating that schools with smaller student bodies and less racially heterogeneous faculty bodies have higher levels of communal school organization.

Student/teacher ratio has a negative effect on Student Bonding (-.579, p<.01), as does student percent male (-.355, p<.01). This suggests that schools with more students per teacher and a larger percentage of male students have lower levels of student bonding. Both student/teacher ratio and student percent male display nonsignificant effects on School Disorder, suggesting that the negative effects seen in Model One are mediated through Student Bonding.

Student racial heterogeneity has a positive effect on School Disorder (.124, p<.01), suggesting that schools with more racially diverse student bodies have higher levels of school disorder. Finally, neighborhood poverty also has a positive effect on School Disorder (.155, p<.01), indicating that schools located in poorer neighborhoods have higher levels of school disorder.

As in Model 1, the modification index for the path from Communal School Organization to Teacher Victimization is high (50.63). Therefore, Model Three was estimated again with this path freed. In addition, paths found to be nonsignificant in the first estimation were not included in the second estimation.

Figure 11: Results for Model Estimated for Hypothesis 3 (Second Estimation)

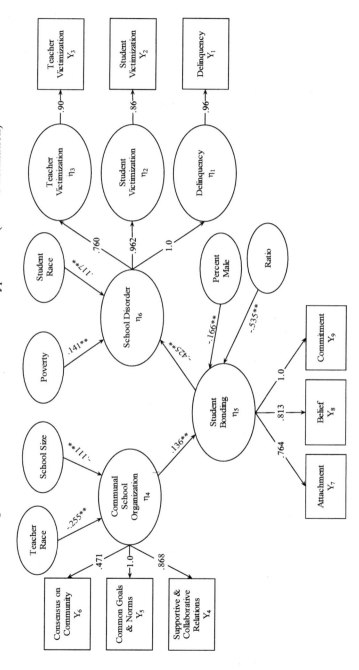

The results of this second estimation can be seen in Figure 11. All paths that were significant in the first estimation are still significant in the second estimation, with minor changes in some values. In addition, the newly freed path is significant. Communal School Organization has a strong negative effect on Teacher Victimization (-.480, p<.01), suggesting that schools that are more communally organized have lower rates of Teacher Victimization. The model has a Chi-Square value of 300.31 (97 degrees of freedom), which is significantly less than the Chi-Square of the first model. This indicates that the model from the second estimation provides a significantly better fit to the data. The GFI for the second estimation is higher (.88), also indicating a better fit to the data.

The results of Model 3 provide support for Hypothesis 3. The path from Communal School Organization to Student Bonding is significant and positive, illustrating that more communally organized schools have higher levels of student bonding. Similarly, the path from Student Bonding to School Disorder is significantand negative, signifying that schools that have higher levels of student bonding have lower levels of school disorder. In the first estimation of Model Three, the path from Communal School Organization to School Disorder was nonsignificant. This indicates that the negative effect Communal School Organization has on School Disorder in Model 1 is mediated through Student Bonding in Model 3, thereby supporting Hypothesis 3. Finally, in the second estimation of Model 3, the direct path from Communal School Organization to Teacher Victimization is significant and negative, indicating that schools that are more communally organized have lower rates of teacher victimization. In addition, this direct path from Communal School Organization to Teacher Victimization is smaller in Model 3, indicating that a portion of the effect seen in Model 1 is mediated by Student Bonding in Model 3. This provides further support for Hypothesis 3.

CHAPTER 5

Interactions among Communal School Organization, School Size, and Racial Diversity: Study Results

HYPOTHESIS FOUR

As discussed in Chapter 3, this study also examined the influence of possible moderating variables. It was hypothesized that communal school organization would interact with school size and racial heterogeneity such that communal organization would have a greater effect on school disorder in larger and more racially diverse schools. To test this hypothesis, School Disorder and each of the separate disorder indicators (Delinquency, Teacher Victimization, and Student Victimization) were first regressed on the interactions between Communal School Organization (CSO) and teacher racial heterogeneity, student racial heterogeneity, student enrollment, and student/teacher ratio. Also included in the regressions were all control variables found to have a significant effect on School Disorder. The results of these regressions can be seen in Tables 21 through 24. The expectation that these interactions would significantly affect school disorder or its indicators was confirmed. The interaction between Communal School Organization and teacher racial heterogeneity has a significant effect on both School Disorder and Teacher Victimization. When student racial heterogeneity was conceptualized using the alternative calculation discussed in Chapter 3, the interaction between Communal School Organization and student racial heterogeneity has a significant effect on School Disorder. The interaction between Communal School Organization and student/teacher ratio has a significant effect on Delinquency, while the interaction between

Table 21: Standardized Regression Coefficients for School Disorder on Interaction Terms (N=305)

Predictor	School Disorder			
CSO-Teacher racial heterogeneity	**-.643**	---	---	---
CSO-Student racial heterogeneity (alternative conceptualization)	---	**-.569***	---	---
CSO-Student/teacher ratio	---	---	-.039	---
CSO-Student enrollment	---	---	---	.236
CSO	-.045	-.004	-.214**	-.246**
Student Bonding	-.569**	-.527**	-.568**	-.577**
Neighborhood poverty	.129*	.235**	.134*	.139*
Student enrollment	-.041	-.168**	-.043	-.277
Student racial heterogeneity	.142**	.713**	.123*	.131*
Student/teacher ratio	.015	.121*	-.054	.022
Student percent male	.079	.036	.062	.065
Teacher racial heterogeneity	.669**	-.071	.010	.009

**p<.01, *p<.05

Table 22: Standardized Regression Coefficients for Teacher
Victimization on Interaction Terms (N=305)

Predictor	Teacher Victimization			
CSO-Teacher racial heterogeneity	-.548**	---	---	---
CSO-Student racial heterogeneity	---	.053	---	---
CSO-Student/teacher ratio	---	---	-.307	---
CSO-Student enrollment	---	---	---	.221
CSO	-.270**	-.423**	-.290**	-.464**
Student Bonding	-.195**	-.201**	-.232**	-.202**
Neighborhood poverty	.210**	.217**	.227**	.218**
Student enrollment	.093	.090	.079	-.128
Student racial heterogeneity	.086	.023	.078	.077
Student/teacher ratio	.021	.030	.304**	.026
Student percent male	.000	-.012	-.010	-.013
Teacher racial heterogeneity	.621*	.058	.058	.059

**p<.01, *p<.05

Table 23: Standardized Regression Coefficients for Delinquency on
Interaction Terms (N=305)

Predictor	Delinquency			
CSO-Teacher racial heterogeneity	-.436	---	---	---
CSO-Student racial heterogeneity	---	-.279	---	---
CSO-Student/teacher ratio	---	---	-.392**	---
CSO-Student enrollment	---	---	---	-.286
CSO	.151*	.129	-.108*	.107
Student Bonding	-.681**	-.690**	-.650**	-.686**
Neighborhood poverty	.080	.086	.074	.084
Student enrollment	-.121**	-.128**	-.112*	.156
Student racial heterogeneity	.129**	.375	.108*	.109*
Student/teacher ratio	-.003	.002	-.328**	.009
Student percent male	.095*	.075	.079	.081
Teacher racial heterogeneity	.451	-.009	-.014	-.015

**p<.01, *p<.05

Table 24: Standardized Regression Coefficients for Student
Victimization on Interaction Terms (N=305)

Predictor	Student Victimization			
CSO-Teacher racial heterogeneity	-.306	---	---	---
CSO-Student racial heterogeneity (alternative conceptualization)	---	-.078	---	---
CSO-Student/teacher ratio	---	---	.048	---
CSO-Student enrollment	---	---	---	**1.064**
CSO	.049	.003	-.042	-.317**
Student Bonding	-.256**	-.260**	-.255**	-.263**
Neighborhood poverty	-.063	-.059	-.061	-.050
Student enrollment	-.047	-.051	-.048	-1.093**
Student racial heterogeneity	.085	.149	.076	.104
Student/teacher ratio	.024	.028	-.012	.014
Student percent male	.081	.071	.073	.079
Teacher racial heterogeneity	.281	-.031	-.032	-.035

**p<.01, *p<.05

Communal School Organization and student enrollment has a significant effect on Student Victimization.

To examine the nature of these interactions, one individual part of the interaction term was split at the 50th percentile and the outcome variable was regressed on the other part of the interaction term along with the control variables. The process is then conducted again, with the other part of the interaction term being split at the 50th percentile. For example, to examine the effect of the interaction between Communal School Organization and teacher racial heterogeneity on School Disorder, the data were split at the 50th percentile value for Communal School Organization. Then School Disorder was regressed on teacher racial heterogeneity and the control variables for the subsample of data for which the value for Communal School Organization is equal to or higher than the 50th percentile value, and again for the subsample of data for which the value of Communal School Organization is lower than the 50th percentile value. The significance and value of teacher racial heterogeneity in each equation was examined. In addition, a t-test was conducted using the unstandardized coefficients and standard errors to test whether the coefficients for teacher racial heterogeneity are significantly different in the two equations. This test statistic is:

$$t = (b_1 - b_2)/(\text{standard error}_1^2 + \text{standard error}_2^2)^{1/2}$$

Next, the data were split at the 50th percentile value for teacher racial heterogeneity. Then School Disorder was regressed on Communal School Organization and the control variables for the subsample of data for which the value for teacher racial heterogeneity is equal to or higher than the 50th percentile value, and again on the subsample of data for which the value of teacher racial heterogeneity is lower than the 50th percentile value. In this case, the significance and value of Communal School Organization was examined and the t-test presented above was conducted on the unstandardized coefficients for Communal School Organization. This process was conducted for each interaction term found to be significant for each outcome variable.

The effect of the interaction between Communal School Organization and teacher racial heterogeneity on School Disorder was examined, following the above process. When the data were split at the 50th percentile of Communal School Organization, the effect of teacher

Table 25: Regression Coefficients for School Disorder on Interaction between Communal School Organization and Teacher Racial Heterogeneity with Communal School Organization split at the 50th percentile

Predictor	High Communal School Organization (N=153)			Low Communal School Organization (N=152)		
	Unstandardized		Standard-ized	Unstandardized		Standard-ized
	Beta	St. Error	Beta	Beta	St. Error	Beta
Communal School Organization	-.16	.11	-.10	-.09	.05	-.12
Teacher racial heterogeneity	**-1.26**	**1.61**	**-.07**	**1.34**	**.96**	**.10**
Student enrollment	1.63x E-04	.00	.06	.00	.00	-.13*
Student/ teacher ratio	-.03	.02	-.11	.02	.01	.12
Student racial heterogeneity	1.94	1.42	.11	2.15	.91	.15*
Percent student male	.00	.01	.03	.02	.01	.18**
Student Bonding	-.63	.08	-.61**	-.50	.06	-.55**
Neighborhood poverty	.07	.14	.04	.35	.09	.26**

**p<.01, *p<.05

racial heterogeneity on School Disorder is nonsignificant both in schools with high levels of Communal School Organization and schools with low levels of Communal School Organization (Table 25). However, the results of the t-test show that the difference between the coefficients approaches statistical significance (1.38, p<.10), with teacher racial heterogeneity showing a negative effect on School Disorder in schools with high levels of Communal School Organization and a positive effect on School Disorder in schools with low levels of Communal School Organization.

When the data were at the 50th percentile of teacher racial heterogeneity, an even stronger difference is found (Table 26). In schools with low teacher racial heterogeneity, Communal School Organization has a nonsignificant effect on School Disorder. However, in the schools with high teacher racial heterogeneity, Communal School Organization has a significant negative effect on School Disorder (-.29, p<.01). The results of the t-test confirm this significant difference between coefficients (2.81, p<.01). That is, for schools with higher levels of teacher racial heterogeneity, those that are more communally organized will have less school disorder than those that are less communally organized. The finding that Communal School Organization significantly affects School Disorder only in schools with higher teacher racial heterogeneity levels suggests that Communal School Organization has a stronger effect in more racially diverse schools.

Similar findings can be seen in Table 27, when the effect of the interaction between Communal School Organization and teacher racial heterogeneity on Teacher Victimization was examined. The data were first split at the 50th percentile of Communal School Organization. The effect of teacher racial heterogeneity on Delinquency is nonsignificant in schools with levels of Communal School Organization equal to or above the 50th percentile value. However, in schools with levels lower than the 50th percentile values, teacher racial heterogeneity has a significant positive effect on Teacher Victimization (.21, p<.05). Again, a t-test confirms this significant difference (2.02, p<.05). This indicates that, in less communally organized schools, a more racially diverse faculty is associated with higher teacher victimization.

When the data were split at the 50th percentile of teacher racial heterogeneity, more significant differences were found (Table 28). In

Table 26: Regression Coefficients for School Disorder on Interaction between Communal School Organization and Teacher Racial Heterogeneity with Teacher Racial Heterogeneity split at the 50th percentile

Predictor	High Teacher Racial Heterogeneity (N=157)			Low Teacher Racial Heterogeneity (N=148)		
	Unstandardized		Standard -ized	Unstandardized		Standard -ized
	Beta	St. Error	Beta	Beta	St. Error	Beta
Communal School Organization	-.16	.04	-.30**	.00	.05	.00
Teacher racial heterogeneity	.50	1.44	.02	-.43	4.98	-.01
Student enrollment	-2.13x E-04	.00	-.08	1.39x E-04	.00	-.05
Student/ teacher ratio	.01	.01	.04	-.02	.02	-.06
Student racial heterogeneity	1.41	1.11	.08	3.60	1.34	.21**
Percent student male	.02	.01	.12	.01	.01	.05
Student Bonding	-.61	.07	-.58**	-.52	.07	-.58**
Neighborhood poverty	.17	.10	.12	.32	.16	.15

**p<.01, *p<.05

Table 27: Regression Coefficients for Teacher Victimization on Interaction between Communal School Organization and Teacher Racial Heterogeneity with Communal School Organization split at the 50th percentile

	High Communal School Organization (N=153)			Low Communal School Organization (N=152)		
	Unstandardized		Standard -ized	Unstandardized		Standard -ized
Predictor	Beta	St. Error	Beta	Beta	St. Error	Beta
Communal School Organization	-.14	.05	-.24**	-.09	.03	-.24**
Teacher racial heterogeneity	**-.52**	**.70**	-.07	**1.43**	**.67**	**.21***
Student enrollment	2.47x E-04	.00	.21*	1.54x E-06	.00	.00
Student/ teacher ratio	.00	.01	-.03	.01	.01	.05
Student racial heterogeneity	.94	.62	.14	.14	.63	.02
Percent student male	-.01	.00	-.11	.01	.01	.18*
Student Bonding	-.15	.03	-.37**	-.03	.04	-.07
Neighborhood poverty	.13	.06	.20*	.20	.06	.29**

**p<.01, *p<.05

Table 28: Regression Coefficients for Teacher Victimization on Interaction between Communal School Organization and Teacher Racial Heterogeneity with Teacher Racial Heterogeneity split at the 50th percentile

Predictor	High Teacher Racial Heterogeneity (N=157)			Low Teacher Racial Heterogeneity (N=148)		
	Unstandardized		Standard-ized	Unstandardized		Standard-ized
	Beta	St. Error	Beta	Beta	St. Error	Beta
Communal School Organization	-.13	.02	-.47**	-.08	.02	-.31**
Teacher racial heterogeneity	.44	.82	.05	-.95	2.32	-.03
Student enrollment	1.10x E-04	.00	.09	1.94x E-04	.00	.15
Student/ teacher ratio	.00	.01	-.01	.01	.01	.05
Student racial heterogeneity	-.27	.64	.03	1.29	.62	.17*
Percent student male	.00	.01	.05	.00	.00	-.06
Student Bonding	-.11	.04	-.21**	-.07	.03	-.18*
Neighborhood poverty	.08	.05	.12	.37	.08	.39**

**p<.01, *p<.05

schools with high levels of teacher racial heterogeneity, the effect of Communal School Organization on Teacher Victimization is significant and negative (-.48, p<.01). In schools with low levels of teacher racial heterogeneity, Communal School Organization also has a significant and negative effect on Teacher Victimization (-.31, p<.01). However, the difference in size between the two unstandardized coefficients approaches statistical significance (1.38, p<.01), leading one to conclude that Communal School Organization has a stronger effect on Teacher Victimization in schools with higher levels of teacher racial heterogeneity.

Again, similar findings were obtained when the effect of the interaction between Communal School Organization and student racial heterogeneity on School Disorder was examined (Table 29). The data were first split at the 50th percentile of Communal School Organization. The effect of student racial heterogeneity on School Disorder is nonsignificant in schools with levels of Communal School Organization equal to or above the 50th percentile value. However, in schools with levels lower than the 50th percentile values, student racial heterogeneity has a significant positive effect on School Disorder (.21, p<.01). This indicates that, in less communally organized schools, a more racially diverse student body is associated with more school disorder.

When the data were split at the 50th percentile of student racial heterogeneity, an even stronger difference is found (Table 30). In schools with low student racial heterogeneity, Communal School Organization has a nonsignificant effect on School Disorder. However, in the schools with high student racial heterogeneity, Communal School Organization has a significant negative effect on School Disorder (-.26, p<.01). The results of the t-test confirm this significant differences between coefficients (2.45, p<.01). That is, for schools with higher levels of student racial heterogeneity, those that are more communally organized will have less school disorder than those that are less communally organized. The finding that Communal School Organization significantly affects School Disorder only in schools with higher student racial heterogeneity levels suggests that Communal School Organization has a stronger effect in more racially diverse schools.

Table 29: Regression Coefficients for School Disorder on Interaction between Communal School Organization and Student Racial Heterogeneity with Communal School Organization split at the 50th percentile

Predictor	High Communal School Organization (N=153)			Low Communal School Organization (N=152)		
	Unstandardized		Standard -ized	Unstandardized		Standard -ized
	Beta	St. Error	Beta	Beta	St. Error	Beta
Communal School Organization	-.09	.11	-.07	-.06	.05	-.09
Teacher racial heterogeneity	-2.53	1.79	-.15	.20	1.06	.02
Student enrollment	-2.24x E-04	.00	-.09	-4.70x E-04	.00	-.19**
Student/ teacher ratio	.00	.03	-.01	.03	.01	.15*
Student racial heterogeneity	**.54**	**.60**	**.10**	**1.15**	**.38**	**.21****
Percent student male	-.01	.01	-.08	.03	.01	.17*
Student Bonding	-.55	.08	-.60**	-.44	.06	-.48**
Neighborhood poverty	.33	.15	.21*	.42	.11	.26**

**p<.01, *p<.05

Table 30: Regression Coefficients for School Disorder on Interaction between Communal School Organization and Student Racial Heterogeneity with Student Racial Heterogeneity split at the 50th percentile

| Predictor | High Student Racial Heterogeneity (N=128) | | | Low Student Racial Heterogeneity (N=128) | | |
| | Unstandardized | | Standard-ized | Unstandardized | | Standard-ized |
	Beta	St. Error	Beta	Beta	St. Error	Beta
Communal School Organization	-.13	.04	-.26**	.00	.04	.00
Teacher racial heterogeneity	-2.06	1.17	-.13	.68	1.53	.04
Student enrollment	-5.47x E-04	.00	-.21	-3.00x E-04	.00	-.14
Student/ teacher ratio	.03	.02	.15	.03	.02	.11
Student racial heterogeneity	1.22	.63	.13	-.12	1.60	-.01
Percent student male	.01	.01	.07	.00	.01	-.01
Student Bonding	-.56	.08	-.54**	-.44	.07	-.57**
Neighborhood poverty	.40	.11	.26**	.19	.18	.10

**p<.01, *p<.05

Table 31: Regression Coefficients for Delinquency on Interaction
between Communal School Organization and Student-Teacher Ratio
with Communal School Organization split at the 50th percentile

Predictor	High Communal School Organization (N=153)			Low Communal School Organization (N=152)		
	Unstandardized		Standard-ized	Unstandardized		Standard-ized
	Beta	St. Error	Beta	Beta	St. Error	Beta
Communal School Organization	.06	.06	.07	-.03	.03	-.05
Teacher racial heterogeneity	-.15	.85	-.01	-.36	.57	-.04
Student enrollment	-1.31x E-04	.00	-.07	-.17x E-04	.00	-.11
Student/ teacher ratio	-.03	.01	-.18*	.02	.01	.15*
Student racial heterogeneity	.80	.74	.08	1.17	.54	.13*
Percent student male	-.01	.01	.07	.01	.01	.10
Student Bonding	-.41	.04	-.67**	-.39	.03	-.69**
Neighborhood poverty	.00	.07	.00	.16	.05	.19**

**p<.01, *p<.05

To examine the effect of the interaction between Communal School Organization and student/teacher ratio on Delinquency, the data were first split at the 50th percentile value for Communal School Organization (Table 31). In schools with high levels of Communal School Organization, the effect of student/teacher ratio on Delinquency is significant and negative (-18, p<.05). However, in schools with low levels of Communal School Organization, the effect of student/teacher ratio on Delinquency is significant and positive (.15, p<.05). The results of the t-test confirm this significant difference (3.46, p<.01). This indicates that a greater ratio of students to teachers actually decreases school disorder in more communally organized schools, while a greater ratio increases school disorder in less communally organized schools. When the data were split at the 50th percentile value of student/teacher ratio (Table 32), the effect of Communal School Organization on Delinquency is nonsignificant in both sets of schools, and the difference between the unstandardized coefficients was nonsignificant.

The finding that a greater ratio between students and teachers actually decreases delinquency in more communally organized schools is perplexing. One possible reason for this finding is the inclusion of behavioral alternative schools in the sample. These are schools to which students with severe behavioral problems are sent; these types of schools generally have small student-teacher ratios. Therefore, within the communally organized schools, those alternative schools that have smaller student-teacher ratios are more likely to have greater rates of delinquency. To examine this possibility, the 26 schools in the sample classified as alternative were removed, and the interaction was re-analyzed. Using this new subsample, the interaction between Communal School Organization and Student-Teacher Ratio was still significant (-.01, p<.05). The data were split at the 50th percentile value for Communal School Organization (Table 33). In schools with high levels of Communal School Organization, the effect of student/teacher ratio on Delinquency is nonsignificant. However, in schools with low levels of Communal School Organization, the effect of student/teacher ratio on Delinquency is significant and positive (.29, p<.01). This indicates that, once alternative schools are removed from the sample, student-teacher ratio is not related to delinquency in more communally organized schools.

Table 32: Regression Coefficients for Delinquency on Interaction between Communal School Organization and Student-Teacher Ratio with Student-Teacher Ratio split at the 50th percentile

Predictor	High Student-Teacher Ratio (N=127)			Low Student-Teacher Ratio (N=127)		
	Unstandardized		Standard -ized	Unstandardized		Standard -ized
	Beta	St. Error	Beta	Beta	St. Error	Beta
Communal School Organization	.00	.02	.00	.02	.03	.06
Teacher racial heterogeneity	-.89	.64	-.10	.46	.75	.04
Student enrollment	-1.02x E-04	.00	-.07	-1.60x E-04	.00	-.09
Student/ teacher ratio	.02	.01	.18**	-.03	.02	-.08
Student racial heterogeneity	.84	.58	.09	1.49	.65	.14*
Percent student male	.00	.01	-.02	.01	.01	.16*
Student Bonding	-.39	.04	-.68**	-.42	.04	-.68**
Neighborhood poverty	.13	.05	.18*	.04	.08	.03

**p<.01, *p<.05

Table 33: Regression Coefficients for Delinquency on Interaction between Communal School Organization and Student-Teacher Ratio with Communal School Organization split at the 50th percentile for sample without alternative schools

Predictor	High Communal School Organization (N=153)			Low Communal School Organization (N=152)		
	Unstandardized		Standard-ized	Unstandardized		Standard-ized
	Beta	St. Error	Beta	Beta	St. Error	Beta
Communal School Organization	.07	.06	.13	-.03	.02	-.06
Teacher racial heterogeneity	-.05	.78	.07	-.93	.53	-.11
Student enrollment	-1.38x E-04	.00	-.11	-1.50x E-04	.00	-.13*
Student/ teacher ratio	-.01	.01	-.11	.01	.00	.29**
Student racial heterogeneity	.02	.70	.00	1.14	.48	.13*
Percent student male	.00	.00	.04	.01	.01	.08
Student Bonding	-.34	.04	-.66**	-.36	.03	-.65**
Neighborhood poverty	.00	.07	.00	.12	.06	.12*

**p<.01, *p<.05

Table 34: Regression Coefficients for Student Victimization on Interaction between Communal School Organization and Student Enrollment with Communal School Organization split at the 50th percentile

Predictor	High Communal School Organization (N=153)			Low Communal School Organization (N=152)		
	Unstandardized		Standard -ized	Unstandardized		Standard -ized
	Beta	St. Error	Beta	Beta	St. Error	Beta
Communal School Organization	-.07	.04	-.16	.03	.02	.13
Teacher racial heterogeneity	-.59	.58	-.10	.27	.40	.07
Student enrollment	**.05**	**.09**	**.05**	**-.16**	**.06**	**-.23****
Student/ teacher ratio	.00	.01	.03	.00	.01	.02
Student racial heterogeneity	.19	.51	.04	.83	.37	.21
Percent student male	.00	.00	.12	.00	.00	.07
Student Bonding	-.07	.03	-.23*	-.08	.02	-.33**
Neighborhood poverty	-.06	.05	-.12	.00	.04	-.01

**p<.01, *p<.05

Table 35: Regression Coefficients for Student Victimization on Interaction between Communal School Organization and Student Enrollment with Student Enrollment split at the 50th percentile

	High Student Enrollment (N=153)			Low Student Enrollment (N=152)		
	Unstandardized		Standard -ized	Unstandardized		Standard -ized
Predictor	Beta	St. Error	Beta	Beta	St. Error	Beta
Communal School Organization	.02	.01	.12	-.02	.02	-.12
Teacher racial heterogeneity	.58	.42	.14	-.55	.52	-.11
Student enrollment	-.28	.08	-.34**	.41	.21	.19**
Student/ teacher ratio	.01	.01	.09	-.01	.01	-.07
Student racial heterogeneity	.28	.40	.06	.60	.45	.12
Percent student male	.00	.00	.08	.00	.00	.08
Student Bonding	-.04	.03	-.17*	-.09	.03	-.30**
Neighborhood poverty	-.01	.03	-.03	-.06	.05	-.11

**p<.01, *p<.05

Finally, to examine the effect of the interaction between Communal School Organization and student enrollment on Student Victimization, the data were first split at the 50th percentile value for Communal School Organization (Table 34). In schools with high levels of Communal School Organization, the effect of student enrollment on Student Victimization is nonsignificant. However, in schools with low levels of Communal School Organization, student enrollment has a significant and negative effect on Student Victimization (-.23, p<.01), indicating that the size of a student body only decreases student victimization in schools that are less communally organized. When the data were split at the 50th percentile value of student enrollment, the effect of Communal School Organization on Student Victimization is nonsignificant in both sets of schools (Table 35). However, the results of the t-test show that the difference between the unstandardized coefficients is significant (1.79, p<..05), with Communal School Organization showing a negative effect in larger schools.

Hypothesis 4 was partially supported. Teacher racial heterogeneity interacts with Communal School Organization such that Communal School Organization displays a stronger negative effect on School Disorder and Teacher Victimization in schools with more racially diverse faculties. Similarly, student racial heterogeneity interacts with Communal School Organization such that Communal School Organization displays a stronger negative effect on School Disorder in schools with more racially diverse student bodies. Finally, student enrollment interacts with Communal School Organization such that Communal School Organization displays a negative effect on Student Victimization in larger schools. However, the findings regarding the interactions between Communal School Organization and student/teacher ratio did not support the hypothesis. Communal School Organization has the same effect on Delinquency regardless of the ratio of students to teachers. The difference for this interaction is found in the effect student/teacher ratio has on Delinquency, depending on the level of Communal School Organization. That is, the ratio between students and teachers negatively affects delinquency in schools that are more communally organized and positively affects delinquency in schools that are less communally organized.

CHAPTER 6

Discussion

SUMMARY OF FINDINGS

This study first examined the measurement models estimated for the latent variables Communal School Organization and Student Bonding and concluded that the measurable scales are accurate indicators of their corresponding latent variables. That is, Supportive and Collaborative Relations, Common Goals and Norms, and Consensus on Community are indeed true indicators of Communal School Organization, while Attachment, Belief, and Commitment are true indicators of Student Bonding. Based on the factor analysis shown in Table Six, however, it is clear that the components of Communal School Organization are not completely distinct factors. To a lesser extent, the same can be said about the components of Student Bonding, based on the factor analysis shown in Table 9.

The measurement model for School Disorder was also examined, with the conclusion that Delinquency, Student Victimization, and Teacher Victimization are all true indicators of School Disorder. This measurement model also provides support to the idea that these three indicators not only share a common underlying construct, but that they also have unique elements that may be affected differently by other variables.

Hypothesis 1, that schools with higher levels of communal school organization have lower rates of school disorder, is supported by Model One. Communal School Organization has a significant negative effect on School Disorder, indicating that schools that are more communally organized do have lower levels of school disorder. When a separate path from Communal School Organization to Teacher Victimization was estimated, this new direct path to Teacher Victimization is significant and negative, indicating that schools that are more communally organized have lower levels of teacher victimization. When this path is estimated, the direct path from Communal School Organization to School Disorder remains significant and negative, although it becomes smaller in size.

Hypothesis 2, that schools with higher levels of communal school organization have higher levels of student bonding, is supported by the results of Model Two. Communal School Organization has a significant positive effect on Student Bonding, which indicates that schools that are more communally organized have higher levels of student bonding.

Hypothesis 3, that the effect of Communal School Organization on School Disorder is mediated through Student Bonding, is supported by Model Three. Communal School Organization has significant positive effect on Student Bonding, suggesting that schools that are more communally organized have higher levels of student bonding. In addition, Student Bonding has a significant negative effect on School Disorder, which suggests that schools with higher levels of student bonding have lower rates of delinquency and victimization. Finally, Communal School Organization has a nonsignificant effect on School Disorder, indicating that the negative effect seen in Model 1 is mediated through Student Bonding. In the second estimate, when a direct path from Communal School Organization to Teacher Victimization is estimated, this path is significant, negative, and smaller than the same path in Model 1, again indicating that some of the negative effect seen in Model 1 is mediated through Student Bonding.

All of the structural equation models also provide significant findings with regard to the control variables. A school's level of communal school organization is affected by the racial heterogeneity of the faculty and the size of the student body, while a school's level of student bonding is influenced by the school's student/teacher ratio and the proportion of the student body that is male. The level of disorder in a school is affected by the racial heterogeneity of the study body and the level of poverty in the surrounding neighborhood. School disorder is also influenced by the percentage of the student body that is male and the student-teacher ratio in the school, although these effects become nonsignificant once student bonding is introduced into the model.

Hypothesis 4 is partially supported. The interactions between Communal School Organization and student racial heterogeneity, teacher racial heterogeneity, student/teacher ratio, and student enrollment were examined and significant results were found. The interaction between Communal School Organization and teacher racial heterogeneity significantly affects both School Disorder and Teacher Victimization. When this interaction was examined further, it was determined that Communal School Organization has a stronger negative effect on School Disorder and Teacher Victimization in schools with higher levels of teacher racial heterogeneity than in schools with lower levels of teacher racial heterogeneity. Similarly, the interaction between Communal School Organization and student racial heterogeneity significantly affects School Disorder such that Communal School Organization has a stronger negative effect on School Disorder in schools with higher levels of student racial heterogeneity than in schools with lower levels of student racial heterogeneity. Finally, the interaction between Communal School Organization and student enrollment was significant. When this interaction was explored further, it was found that Communal School Organization had a negative effect on Student Victimization in larger schools. These findings support Hypothesis Four. However, the findings regarding the interactions between Communal School Organization and student/teacher ratio do not support the hypothesis. Communal School Organization has the same effect on Delinquency regardless of the ratio of students to teachers. Instead, the ratio between students and teachers negatively affects delinquency in schools that are more communally organized and positively affects delinquency in schools that are less communally organized.

DISCUSSION OF FINDINGS

The majority of the findings in this study support the hypotheses set forth in Chapter 2. Communal school organization reduces school disorder and increases student bonding. In addition, student bonding reduces school disorder, and mediates some of the negative effect communal school organization has on school disorder. Finally, the effect of communal school organization on school disorder is greater in schools that are racially heterogeneous. All of these findings are not surprising, as they are suggested by the studies discussed in the literature review in Chapter 2.

Also not surprising are the majority of findings regarding the control variables. It is logical that levels of communal school organization are lower in larger schools. More students will make the development of a sense of community more difficult by hindering the development of supportive relations between teachers and students and among the student body, by reducing the amount of opportunities for all members to engage in active participation and collaboration, and by inhibiting the development of a set of goals and values shared by all school members. Bryk and Driscoll (1988) also found a negative association between school size and communal school organization. The finding that schools with greater student-teacher ratios have lower levels of student bonding is also expected. A teacher that is responsible for more students will be less able to create a strong attachment with all students, thereby leading to lower levels of student bonding. Another expected finding is that schools with great student/teacher ratios will experience more disorder. If teachers are responsible for more students, their supervision will be less effective and the students will have more opportunities to engage in delinquency. Finally, it was expected that more neighborhood poverty, a more heterogeneous student body, and a higher percentage of male students would lead to more school disorder; previous research predicts all of these associations (Federal Bureau of Investigation, 2000; Johnston, O'Malley, and Bachman, 2002; Johnson, 1992; Sampson, 1999).

One interesting finding in the first model is that communal school organization has a separate effect on teacher victimization that is stronger than the effect it has on school disorder. That is, when the direct effect from communal school organization to teacher victimization was estimated, the effect from communal school organization to the full school disorder construct became smaller in size. The most likely explanation for this finding is methodological. The items used to operationalize both communal school organization and teacher victimization are from the teacher survey, while the items used to operationalize student victimization and delinquency are from the student survey. Therefore, it seems that items from the same survey are more likely to correlate, leading communal school organization to have a stronger association with teacher victimization than with student victimization or delinquency. If this study contained measures of communal school organization from the student point-of-view, communal school organization would most likely have an effect on all indicators of school disorder.

Another interesting finding is the inverse association between communal school organization and the racial heterogeneity of the faculty: schools with more racially heterogeneous faculty bodies are less communally organized. This finding is not unexpected; Bryk and Driscoll (1988) also found lower levels of communal school organization in schools that are more ethnically or racially diverse. One possible explanation for this relationship is the existence of goals and norms that are shared by the community in the school. Schools that are more racially heterogeneous may have conflicting sets of goals and norms among the faculty and the student body, thereby leading the school to be less communally organized. As Bryk and Driscoll (1988) state, "It would seem easier to sustain a communal organizational life when the institution attracts like-minded individuals" (p. 18). Related to this is the possibility that schools that emphasize community could neglect or stigmatize individuality, and thereby devalue diversity (Fullan and Hargreaves, 1996). This suggests a negative aspect of communal school organization: the possibility that diversity is disadvantageous to the social organization, delinquency, and victimization in a school. Taken to its logical yet absurd extreme, this association seems to suggest that schools should be racially segregated, thereby resulting in higher levels of communal school organization and lower levels of delinquency and victimization. However, the more likely suggestion deals, again, with the scope and content of the shared goals and norms. In a heterogeneous school, agreement may only be needed on a small group of core goals and norms, with diversity allowed on the larger set of less important goals and norms (Bryk and Driscoll, 1988). For instance, one of the core values of the school should be an appreciation of multicultural diversity. A shared focus on the positive aspects of the heterogeneity within a school would counteract the negative effect of that heterogeneity on the communal organization of that school. Diversity would then be acceptable on the larger set of goals, such as focus on different extra-curricular activities or trajectories of study.

Examination of the significant interaction terms provides more detail on the relationship between communal school organization and student and teacher racial heterogeneity. Communal school organization reduces school disorder and teacher victimization more in racially heterogeneous schools than in racially homogeneous schools. The most likely explanation for this finding deals with the negative association between communal school organization and racial heterogeneity discussed in the above paragraph. Since it is less likely for racially heterogeneous schools to develop a strong community, those schools that do develop these communities are more likely to see even greater reductions in disorder. In other words, if racially diverse schools do achieve high levels of communal school organization, the effect of communal school organization on school disorder is actually stronger in these schools than in more homogeneous schools. Therefore, it appears that the strength of communal school organization can buffer the negative effect that heterogeneity has on school disorder. Although racial heterogeneity can increase school disorder, communal school organization can counteract this increase by focusing on the communal aspects of the school. Again, this is related to the role of individuality within community. Instead of focusing on the differences in a negative light, school members will focus on the greater community which values of diversity, thereby improving the social organization and level of disorder in the school.

Finally, the examination of the interaction between student/teacher ratio and communal school organization yielded interesting findings. It was found that student-teacher ratio negatively affects delinquency in schools that are more communally organized and positively affects delinquency in schools that are less communally organized. That is, a greater ratio between students and teachers actually reduces delinquency in schools that are more communally organized but increases delinquency in schools that are less communally organized. The finding that greater student-teacher ratios increase delinquency in schools that are not communally organized is logical. More students per teacher would lead to less effective supervision and more delinquent opportunities. In addition, schools that are not communally organized will have lower levels of student bonding, also leading to more delinquency. The perplexing finding with this interaction is that, in schools that are more communally organized, greater student-teacher ratios actually decrease delinquency. However, this finding is likely driven by the inclusion of alternative schools in the sample. These are schools to which students who have been expelled from regular schools are sent; these types of schools generally have small student-teacher ratios. Therefore, within the communally organized schools, those alternative schools that have smaller student-teacher ratios are more likely to have greater rates of delinquency. When schools that were classified as behavioral alternative schools were removed from the sample, this perplexing finding did, in fact, disappear. That is, once alternative schools were removed, student-teacher ratio had a nonsignificant effect on delinquency in more communally organized schools.

LIMITATIONS OF STUDY

As with all research, there are some limitations to this study. The most important limitation is the cross-sectional nature of the data. Because all data were collected at the same time, it is impossible to truly determine the causal direction of the associations found in this study. For instance, the negative association between communal school organization and victimization could indicate that a strong sense of community in school leads to less victimization, as predicted by the hypotheses. However, it could also indicate that lower victimization rates lead to a strong sense of community or that the relationship between the two constructs is reciprocal. Furthermore, the wording in the survey would seem to suggest a causal order that is the opposite from what is predicted by this study: The delinquency and victimization items are worded such that they measure activity in the twelve months prior to the survey, while the community and bonding items measure those factors at the time of the survey.

The cross-sectional nature of the data would be a larger problem, however, if this study was examining constructs that are not stable over time. However, previous research has demonstrated the time-stable nature of these constructs. For instance, G. Gottfredson (1999) presents the one-year retest reliabilities for student bonding components for student surveys conducted in 1981 and again in 1982. Attachment to school had a retest reliability of .53 for males and .46 for females, while Belief had a retest reliability of .38 for males and .40 for females (G. Gottfredson, 1999). In addition, G. Gottfredson (1999) displays the one-year and two-year stability coefficients for student bonding measures and school climate measures for surveys conducted between the years of 1981 and 1983. Attachment to school had a one-year stability coefficient of .83 and a two-year coefficient of .72, while Belief had a one-year stability coefficient of .59 and a two-year coefficient of .50 (G. Gottfredson, 1999). Morale, a scale upon which the Supportive and Collaborative Relations scale in this study is based, had a one-year stability coefficient of .62 and a two-year coefficient of .65 (G. Gottfredson, 1999). All of these correlations are significant at the p<.01 level (G. Gottfredson, 1999).

Huizinga and Elliot (1986) present similar results with regards to delinquency. They examined the percentage of respondents in low delinquency and high delinquency groups that have a difference between their test and retest scores with a value of two or less, and found that 60% of low delinquency respondents and 20% of high delinquency respondents fall into this category. When specific offenses were examined, the percentages were much higher for both groups, ranging from 51.6% to 100%. Given the low mean of delinquency in this study, one can assume that the majority of respondents would belong in the low delinquency group, and would therefore most likely display a test-retest difference of two or less.

There is no doubt that the cross-sectional nature of the data used in this study certainly presents a major limitation when interpreting the causal order of the results. However, this limitation is less problematic given the relative stability of the constructs examined in this study.

Another important limitation is the low school response rate overall and the relationship between survey participation and community characteristics. Schools in urban areas, with more female-headed households with children, a greater proportion of urban population, and more households that received public assistance were significantly less likely to have participated in the study. Therefore, the study results may not generalize well to schools located in such communities. It is unlikely, however, that the basic results of the study would change had these schools been included. Exploratory analyses of potential biases introduced by the low response rates suggested that participating schools located in similar communities as the majority of non-participating schools were more likely to have lower levels of communal school organization and higher rates of disorder. It therefore seems likely that the inclusion of the non-participating schools would have resulted in actually intensifying the relationships reported in this study. Of course, it is possible that the relationships of interest are not linear in the region of the distribution in which the non-participating schools fall, or that some characteristic unmeasured by the study and related to participation, communal school organization, and school disorder might alter the relationships. However, the linear relationship between the community characteristics related to non-participation and levels of communal school organization and school disorder seem to indicate that, if anything, the results presented here provide conservative estimates of the effect of communal school organization on school disorder. Nevertheless, future research should replicate this study with samples that are more representative of schools in urban, disadvantaged communities.

Another limitation is the lack of data on a variety of issues. For instance, there is no data on parental involvement in the school, which research presents as an important element of the school community (Hawley and Rollie, 2002). By involving the parents in the school community, administrators and faculty ensure continuity in the students' experiences in school and in the home. Unfortunately, the data used in this study do not include information on this important component of communal school organization.

Also missing from the data is information on student academic achievement. As discussed in Chapter 2, another benefit of communal school organization is an improvement in the academic performance of the student body (Bryk and Driscoll, 1988). Having data on academic achievement would allow the addition of another outcome of interest in this study. However, there is a much larger gap in the research regarding the influence of communal school organization on delinquency and victimization.

There is also a lack of student reports on sense of community, which would be helpful in order to further investigate the relationships among communal school organization, student bonding, and school disorder. This would ensure that the communal organization of a school is felt by all members of the community, not just by the adults in the school. This lack of student data on communal school organization is the most likely explanation for the fact that, in this study, communal school organization has a stronger effect on teacher victimization than on student victimization or delinquency.

Also missing from the data are measures of school governance. While this study relies on the elements of communal school organization discussed by Bryk and Driscoll (1988) (system of shared values, common agenda of activities, and ethos of caring), others discuss the importance of participatory governance as an additional element of communal school organization (Battistich et al., 1997; Welsh et al., 1999). In communally organized schools, the planning and decision making are more likely to be influenced by all members of the school community, which is likely to lead to a greater sense of belonging and greater internalization of the common norms and goals.

Finally, as discussed earlier in this chapter, this study lacks information on the content of the shared goals and norms in a communally organized school. While the data include measures of the existence of common goals, norms, and values, they do not include measures of the actual content of these goals, norms, and values. This information would be especially helpful for studying the association between racial heterogeneity and communal school organization, as well as for gathering more in depth information on the different types of communal school organization.

FUTURE RESEARCH AND THEORETICAL DEVELOPMENT

Future studies could alleviate several of the limitations discussed in the above section. To assess proper temporal ordering, future studies should be longitudinal in nature, collecting data on communal school organization, student bonding, delinquency, and victimization at several points in time. Future research should also replicate this study with samples that are more representative of schools in urban, disadvantaged communities. Data should also be collected on parental involvement and academic achievement, thereby adding another component of communal school organization and examining another possible outcome. Future research data could also include additional neighborhood measures. While this study had data on the neighborhood surrounding the school, it would be beneficial to also have data on the neighborhoods in which the students actually live.

Finally, future research should collect sense of community data from student as well as adult members of the school, since having data from all members of the school is the only way to determine if a community truly exists.

Future research should include a multi-level analysis of the concepts included in this study. While communal school organization is clearly a school-level concept, the other constructs in this study, such as student bonding, delinquency, and victimization, should be examined at both the individual-level and the school-level.

Future studies could also examine the relationship between communal school organization and the type of school. For instance, Bryk has examined the existence of communal organization within Catholic schools (Bryk, 1995). It is possible that schools that are more homogeneous by nature, such as Catholic schools or schools with same-sex student bodies, will find greater ease in the creation of a school community. More research could also be conducted on the existence and results of community in behavioral alternative schools, magnet schools, and vocational schools.

In addition, future studies should examine the communal organization of a school in more depth by collecting data not just on the existence of communal organization, but on the type of communal school organization. For instance, research should collect more detailed data on the content of the shared goals, norms, and values of a school. As discussed previously, this study included data on the existence of these shared norms, but not on the content, which has implications for the relationship between teachers and students as well as for the effect of student and teacher racial heterogeneity on the school community. Future research should also explore the relationship between racial heterogeneity and community, as well as the relationship between absolute race (ie: African-American versus Caucasian) and community.

Additionally, more detailed data should be collected on the collaborative relations within the school, in order to assess the professional and social quality of these relations. Fullan and Hargreaves (1996) discuss different types of collaborative relationships, which range from weak collaborative cultures, in which teachers merely engage in storytelling about students, to strong collaborative cultures, in which teachers engage in such joint work as team teaching and peer observation (Fullan and Hargreaves, 1996). Data are also needed on the existence of participatory governance in a school, such as planning and decision making activities by all school members. Data on these types of collaborative relationships and school governance schemes should be collected and the effect of these different types of cultures on delinquency and victimization should be analyzed.

Another aspect of communal school organization that should be examined, both theoretically and in research, is the focus on individuality. It is possible that some types of communally organized schools could neglect or stigmatize individuality, which should not be the true intent of community (Fullan and Hargreaves, 1996). The focus should instead be on creating a community that appreciates individuality and utilizes that individuality to further the good of the community. However, this relationship between the community and the individual needs further theoretical exploration. How does a school encourage community without suppressing individuality and diversity? How does a school encourage individuality and diversity and still retain the commonality of direction that is important to the school community? One possibility that has already been discussed is the inclusion of multicultural and diversity appreciation as one of the core goals for a school community. Another possibility is the encouragement of unique and individual ideas in problem-solving sessions intended to improve the school community, thereby demonstrating the importance of individuality. These and other possibilities about the balance between the community and the individual should be explored further.

Finally, future research should explore the relationship between the theoretical constructs in this study in more detail. For instance, are certain components of communal school organization and student bonding more important than others for the reduction of delinquency and victimization? That is, are common goals and norms and the belief in school rules more likely to reduce delinquency and victimization than supportive and collaborative relations and attachment to teachers, or vice versa? Similarly, do certain components of communal school organization have stronger relationships with certain components of student bonding? It is possible that supportive and collaborative relations are more likely to increase attachment to teachers, due to the emotional aspect of these two components, while common goals and norms are more likely to increase belief in school rules, due to the rational aspect of these two components.

In addition, further exploration of the relationships *among* the elements of communal school organization is necessary. Do these elements occur simultaneously or is there an order in which each element develops? One could envision a process whereby the supportive and collaborative relations found in more communally organized schools leads to a more participatory style of governance, which then affects the creation of common goals and norms. Conversely, it could be that the participatory governance leads to the more supportive relations. Are all elements equally important in affecting school disorder? And are all elements necessary in order to achieve high levels of student bonding? Must supportive relations exist or are common norms and goals sufficient, and vice versa? These questions are similar to the discussion by Sampson and his colleagues on the community-level relationships between social cohesion, collective efficacy, and social control (Sampson, 2001; Morenoff et al., 2001), and lead to the possibility of a misspecification in the definition of communal school organization. *If* each element of communal school organization develops at a different point in time, with one element possibly leading to another, or *if* every element is not necessary to achieve high levels of student bonding and low levels of school disorder, then perhaps these elements are truly independent concepts and should not be linked under one underlying construct. Future research should certainly explore these possibilities.

POTENTIAL FOR PREVENTION

The findings of this study regarding the positive effects of communal school organization have great potential for school-based delinquency prevention. Interventions that can strengthen the communal organization of the school and, in turn, increase student bonding, can lead to reductions in the amount of delinquency and victimization in the school. In addition, interventions that can strengthen communal school organization can counter the negative effect racial heterogeneity has on school disorder.

An example of such an intervention is the School Development Program (SDP), developed by James Comer (Haynes and Comer, 1996). The SDP works to build learning communities in the school through collaboration of parents, school staff, and community members. There are three mechanisms upon which the program is built: the school planning and management team, the student and staff support team, and the parent program. The school planning and management team, the central component of the SDP, works to establish an agenda for the school and to improve the social and academic climate in the school. The student and staff support team works with individual problem students and is also involved in building a positive school community. Finally, the parent program involves parents in social activities, planning activities, and volunteering within the school.

Results of many research studies indicate the effectiveness of the School Development Program (Haynes and Comer, 1996). SDP has demonstrated positive effects of academic achievement, student behavior, and overall student adjustment (Cauce, Comer, and Schwartz, 1987; Haynes and Comer, 1990; Haynes, Comer, and Hamilton-Lee, 1988, 1989). Improvements have also been seen in teacher efficacy and satisfaction (Haynes et al., 1989), as well as in teacher and student assessments of school climate and supportive relations (Haynes and Comer, 1996). Cook, Hunt, and Murphy (1998) also found positive results after evaluating the School Development Program in schools in Chicago. The program resulted in improvements in school social and academic climate, reading and math scores, problem behavior, and attitudes toward misbehavior.

Another example of an intervention which works to improve the community within a school is the Child Development Project, developed by Battistich and his colleagues (Battistich et al., 1996). The Child Development Project is a comprehensive elementary school intervention that helps schools become caring communities. The program creates school environments that are characterized by caring and supportive relations among all school participants, by collaboration and involvement of all school participants, and by shared commitment to common norms and values, including caring, justice, responsibility, and learning (Battistich et al., 1996).

The Child Development Program focuses on five key program dimensions (Battistich et al., 1996). The first is the building of stable, caring, and supportive relationships. The adults in the schools work toward fostering these relationships among the adults, between the adults and the students, and among the students. The second dimension is attention to both social and ethical learning along with intellectual learning. By teaching and modeling caring and principled behavior, the adults in the school help to promote the caring community. Third, teachers focus on teaching problem-solving and exploration skills that apply to the social, ethical, and intellectual learning discussed above. The fourth dimension is a focus on challenging yet learner-centered curriculum; the teachers provide activities that are challenging yet flexible, and relevant to students' lives. Finally, the adults in the school attempt to foster "intrinsic motivation" within the students; in other words, they help the students understand the benefits of a caring community without the use of extrinsic incentives (Battistich et al., 1996). The Child Development Project also provides guidelines for the school's curriculum and pedagogy. The program suggests the use of cooperative learning strategies, a values-rich and literature-based reading and language arts program, developmental discipline techniques, classroom and school community-building activities, and home activities to bridge the gap between home and school (Battistich et al., 1996).

Battistich et al. (1996) examined the effects of the Child Development Program on student outcomes in 24 schools from six school districts. Comparing schools that received the program with comparison schools over time, they found a statistically significant decline in alcohol use in the treatment school and a statistically significant increase in alcohol use in the comparison school. Similar results were found for marijuana use, however the results were not statistically significant. The researchers also examined differences in outcomes between schools with high program implementation, moderate implementation, and low implementation. Not surprisingly, the best results were shown in schools with high implementation quality. These schools exhibited a decline in alcohol use, marijuana use, weapon carrying, vehicle theft, truancy, and violent threats (Battistich et al., 1996).

Other interventions that do not specifically focus on building communities but can still improve the communal nature of a school are programs which create teams of school members for the purpose of improving the school. An example of this type of intervention is PATHE (Positive Action Through Holistic Education), which has been implemented in middle and high schools (D. Gottfredson, 1986). This program focused on building a school's capacity to manage itself through the use of teams composed of teachers, administrators, and students, who worked to improve the overall school climate and the academic performance of all students. D. Gottfredson (1986) found that schools that participated in PATHE experienced improvements in school climate and student bonding, and decreases in delinquency.

Finally, interventions that seek to improve the collaboration and collegiality among school staff can improve the communal nature of a school. Examples of such activities include team teaching and planning, peer observation and coaching, mentoring, and action research. These types of activities create interdependence among teachers and commitment of the collective faculty to improve the school, thereby strengthen the school collaborative culture and community (Little, 1990).

CONCLUSION

The benefits of communal school organization are clear: an increase in student bonding and, in turn, a decrease in school disorder. However, there are some possible downsides of communal school organization to consider. As mentioned previously, it is possible that, when emphasizing community, individuality can be neglected or even labeled as negative (Sampson, 1999). This is not the intention of the focus on community; individuality is necessary for organizational growth and positive problem-solving. Instead, the goal is to create a community that enhances this individuality (Fullan and Hargreaves, 1996). Another caution involves the relationship between the content of common goals and norms and the racial heterogeneity of the faculty and/or the student body. Taken to the extreme, it is possible that racism could become one of the shared values of the school community (Sampson, 1999). To counter this possibility, a school should focus on making appreciation of multicultural diversity one of these shared values.

A more general issue is the acknowledgement that schools are part of a much larger picture (Laub and Lauritsen, 1998). Increasing the levels of communal organization and student bonding of a school will not solve all problems of delinquency and victimization. Institutions such as the family and neighborhood community play a large part in the delinquency and victimization equation and need to be addressed above and beyond their relationship with the school institution.

The findings of this study, however, are applicable to the greater community, in that they relate to Sampson's concept of neighborhood ollective efficacy. As discussed in Chapter One, collective efficacy refers to positive social relations among neighbors in a community as well as the willingness of neighbors to intervene for the good of the community (Sampson et al., 1997). Sampson and his colleagues propose that neighborhoods with higher collective efficacy levels will have higher levels of informal social control, which will then lead to lower levels of crime and delinquency (Sampson et al., 1997). If one equates collective efficacy to communal school organization, and informal social control to student bonding, the results of this study clearly support Sampson's hypotheses.

Helping schools to increase communal organization and student bonding can reduce school disorder. School-based interventions such as the ones described above could result in significant positive outcomes for a school by taking advantage of the benefits of communal school organization. By improving the relationships among school members, the collaboration and participation of these members, and the agreement on common goals and norms, students will become more attached to teachers, more committed to education, and give more legitimacy to school rules and norms. With these improvements in communal organization and student bonding, schools will experience an improvement in school climate and a reduction in delinquency and victimization rates.

REFERENCES

Agnew, R. (1985). Social Control Theory and Delinquency: A Longitudinal Test. *Criminology, 43,* 47-61.

Battistich, V., D. Solomon, D. Kim, M. Watson, and E. Schaps (1995). Schools as communities, poverty levels of student populations, and students' attitudes, motives, and performance: A multilevel analysis. American Educational *Research Journal, 32,* 627-658.

Battistich, V., E. Schaps, M. Watson, and D. Solomon (1996). Prevention effects of the child development project: Early findings from an ongoing multi-site demonstration trial. *Journal of Adolescent Research, 11,* 12-35.

Battistich, V., and A. Hom (1997). The relationship between students' sense of their school as a community and their involvement in problem behavior. *American Journal of Public Health, 87,* 12, 1997-2001.

Battistich, V., and D. Solomon (1997). Caring school communities. *Educational Psychologist, 32,* 3, 137-151

Bird, T., and J. Little (1986). How schools organize the teaching occupation. *Elementary School Journal, 86,* 493-511.

Bollen, K.A. (1989). *Structural Equations with Latent Variables.* NY: Wiley & Sons.

Botvin, G.J., S. Schinke, and M.A. Orlandi (1995). School-based health promotion: Substance abuse and sexual behavior. *Applied and Preventive Psychology, 4,* 167-184.

Brooks, K., Schiraldi, V., and Ziedenberg, J. (2000). *School House Hype: Two Years Later.* Justice Policy Institute and Children's Law Center, Inc. Washington, D.C.

Bryk, A.S. (1995). Lessons from Catholic High Schools on Renewing our Educational Institutions. In M.T. Hallinan (ed.), *Restructuring Schools: Promising Practices and Policies.* New York: Plenum Press.

Bryk, A.S., and M.E. Driscoll (1988). The school as community: Shaping forces and consequences for students and teachers. Madison: University of Wisconsin, National Center on Effective Secondary Schools.

Bryk, A.S., and Y.M. Thum (1989). The effects of high school organization on dropping out: An exploratory investigation. *American Educational Research Journal, 26,* 353-383.

Cernkovich, S., and P. Giordano (1987). Family Relationships and Delinquency. *Criminology, 25,* 295-321.

Chandler, K.A., C.D. Chapman, M.R. Rand, and B.M. Taylor (1998). *Students' reports of school crime: 1989 and 1995* (NCES-98-241/NCJ-169607). Washington, DC: U.S. Department of Education and Justice.

Cook, T.D., H.D. Hunt, and R.F. Murphy (1998). Comer's School Development Program in Chicago: A theory-based evaluation. Working papers. Evanston, IL: Northwestern University Institute for Policy Research.

Corcoran, T.B. (1985). Effective secondary schools. In R.M. Kyle (ed.), *Reaching for excellence: An effective schools sourcebook.* Washington, DC: US Government Printing.

Dewey, J. (1966). *Democracy and Education.* NY: Macmillan.

Duke, D.L. (1989). School organization, leadership, and student behavior. In O.C. Moles (ed.), *Strategies to reduce student behavior* (pp.19-46). Washington, D.C.: U.S. Department of Education.

Elrod, H.P., and P.C. Friday (1986). Milwood alternative education project (supplemental report). Kalamazoo, MI: Western Michigan University, Department of Sociology.

Federal Bureau of Investigation (2000). *Crime in the United States, 2000: Uniform Crime Reports.* Washington, DC: U.S. Department of Justice.

Friday, P.C., and P. Elrod (1983). Delinquency prevention through alternative education: The Milwood project presentation to the

Kalamazoo Board of Education, March 24. Kalamazoo, MI: Western Michigan University, Department of Sociology.

Fullan, M.G. (1985). Change Processes and Strategies at the Local Level. *The Elementary School Journal, 85*, 3, 391-421.

Fullan, M.G., and A. Hargreaves (1996). *What's Worth Fighting for in Your School?* New York: Teachers College Press.

Goodenow, C. (1993a). Classroom belonging among early adolescent students: Relationships to motivation and achievement. *Journal of Early Adolescence, 13*, 21-43.

Goodenow, C (1993b). The psychological sense of school membership among adolescents: Scale development and educational correlates. *Psychology in the Schools, 30*, 79-90.

Gottfredson, D.C. (November, 1986). Increasing Orderliness in Urban Public Schools Through Organizational Change. Paper presented at meeting of the American Society of Criminology, Atlanta, GA.

Gottfredson, D.C. (1986). An Empirical Test of School-Based Environmental and Individual Interventions to Reduce the Risk of Delinquent Behavior. *Criminology, 24*, 4, p. 705-731.

Gottfredson, D.C. (1987). An evaluation of an organization development approach to reducing school disorder. *Evaluation Research, 11*, 739-763.

Gottfredson, D.C. (1990). Developing Effective Organizations to Reduce School Disorder. In O.C. Moles (ed.) *Student Discipline Strategies*. New York: State University of New York Press, Albany.

Gottfredson, D.C. (1997). School-Based Crime Prevention. In L.W. Sherman, D.C. Gottfredson, D. MacKenzie, J. Eck, P. Reuter, and S. Bushway (eds.). Preventing crime: *What works, what doesn't, what's promising: A report to the United States Congress*. Washington, D.C.: U.S. Department of Justice Office of Justice Programs.

Gottfredson, D.C. (2001). *Delinquency and schools*. New York: Cambridge University Press.

Gottfredson, D.C., and M.S. Cook (1986). A Test of a School-Based Program to Reduce Delinquency by Increasing Social Integration: The Milwood Alternative Education Project. Baltimore: Center for Social Organization of Schools, Johns Hopkins University.

Gottfredson, D.C., and G.D. Gottfredson (1992). Theory-guided investigation: Three field experiments. In J. McCord and R. Tremblay (eds.), The prevention of antisocial behavior in children (pp. 311-329). NY: Guillford Press.

Gottfredson, D.C., G.D. Gottfredson, and L.G. Hybl. (1990). Managing adolescent behavior: A multi-year, multi-school study (Report No. 50). Baltimore: Johns Hopkins University, Center for Research on Elementary and Middle Schools.

Gottfredson, D.C., G.D. Gottfredson, and L.G. Hybl. (1993). Managing adolescent behavior: A multi-year, multi-school study. *American Educational Research Journal*, 30, 179-215.

Gottfredson, D.C., D.B. Wilson, and S.S. Najaka (2002). School-based prevention of problem behaviors. In Sherman, Lawrence, David Farrington, Brandon Welsh, and Doris MacKenzie. Evidence-Based Crime Prevention. London, UK: Routledge.

Gottfredson, G.D. (1981). Schooling and delinquency. In S.E. Martin, L.B. Sechrest, and R. Redner (eds.), New directions in the rehabilitation of criminal offenders (pp. 424-469). Washington, D.C.: National Academy Press.

Gottfredson, G.D. (1987). American education – American delinquency. *Today's Delinquent, 6,* 5-70.

Gottfredson, G.D. (1999). User's manual for the Effective School Battery. Ellicot City, MD: Gottfredson Associates. [Originally published in 1984].

Gottfredson, G.D., and D.C. Gottfredson (1985). *Victimization in schools*. New York: Plenum.

Gottfredson, G.D. and D.C. Gottfredson (1987). *Using organizational development to improve school climate* (Report No. 17). Baltimore, MD: Johns Hopkins University, Center for Research on Elementary and Middle Schools. (ERIC No. ED 295 283)

Gottfredson, G.D., and D.C. Gottfredson (1999). *Development and applications of theoretical measures for evaluating drug and delinquency prevention programs: Technical manual for research editions of What About You (WAY).* Ellicot City, MD: Gottfredson Associates.

Gottfredson, G.D., D.C. Gottfredson, E.R. Czeh, D. Cantor, S. Crosse, and I. Hantman (2000). *National Study of Delinquency Prevention in Schools.* Ellicot City: Gottfredson Associates, Inc.

Gottfredson, G.D., D.C. Gottfredson, A.A. Payne, and N. Gottfredson (2004). School Climate Predictors of School Disorder: Results from the National Study of Delinquency Prevention in Schools. (unpublished manuscript).

Gottfredson G.D., and J.L. Holland (1997). EIS Organizational Focus Questionnaire. In J.L. Holland, *Making vocational choices: A theory of vocational personalities and work environments (3rd edition),* pp. 273-275. Odessa, FL: Psychological Assessment Resources.

Grant, J., and F. Capell (1983). Reducing school crime: A report on the school team approach. San Rafael, CA: Social Action Research Center.

Harris, Louis, and Associates (1993). *Violence in America's Public Schools: A Survey of the American Teacher.* New York: Metropolitan Life Insurance Company.

Hawley, W.D. (ed) with D.L. Rollie (2002). *The Keys to Effective Schools.* California: Corwin Press, Inc.

Haynes, N.M., and J.P. Comer (1996). Integrating schools, families, and communities through successful school reform: The school development program. *School Psychology Review, 25, 4,* 501-507.

Heaviside, S., C. Rowand, C. Williams, and E. Farris (1998). *Violence and discipline problems in U.S. public schools: 1996-97* (NCES 98-030). Washington, DC: National Center for Education Statistics, U.S. Department of Education.

Hirschi, T. (1969). *Causes of Delinquency*. Berkeley: University of California Press.

Huizinga, D., and D.S. Elliot (1986). Reassessing the Reliability and Validity of Self-Report Delinquency Measures. *Journal of Quantitative Criminology, Vol. 2,* 4, 293-327.

Ingersoll, R. (2001). Teacher turnover and teacher shortages: An organizational analysis. American Educational Research Journal, 38, 499-534.

Jenkins, P.H. (1997). School delinquency and the school social bond. *Journal of Research in Crime and Delinquency,* 34, 3, 337-368.

Johnson, J. (1992). *Criminal Victimization in the United States.* Washington, DC: Bureau of Justice Statistics.

Johnston, L.D., P.M. O'Malley, and J.G. Bachman (2002). *Monitoring the Future: Overview of Key Findings, 2001.* (NIH Publication No. 02-5105). Bethesda, MD: National Institute on Drug Abuse.

Kaufman, P., X. Chen, S.P. Choy, K. Peter, S.A. Ruddy, A.K. Miller, J.K. Fleury, K.A. Chandler, M.G. Planty, and M.R. Rand. *Indicators of School Crime and Safety: 2001.* U.S. Department of Education and Justice. NCES 2002-113/NCJ-190075. Washington, DC: 2001.

Kelloway, E.K. (1998). *Using LISREL for Structural Equation Modeling.* CA: Sage Publications.

Krohn, M.D., and J.L. Massey (1980). Social control and delinquent behavior: An examination of the elements of the social bond. *The Sociological Quarterly, 21,* 529-544.

Kruse, S.D., K.L. Louis, and A.S. Bryk (1995). An emerging framework for analyzing school-based professional community. In K.S. Louis and S.D. Kruse (eds.) *Professionalism and community: Perspectives on urban educational reform.* Thousand Oaks, CA: Corwin.

LaFree, G. (1998). *Losing Legitimacy: Street Crime and the Decline of Social Institutions in America.* Boulder, CO: Westview Press.

Laub, J.H., and J. L. Lauritsen (1998). The interdependence of school violence with neighborhood and family conditions. In Elliot, D.S., B.A. Hamburg, and K.R. Williams (eds) *Violence in American Schools.* Cambridge, U.K.: Cambridge University Press.

Lawrence, R. (1998). *School Crime and Juvenile Justice.* New York: Oxford University Press, Inc.

Lee, V.E., A.S. Bryk and J.B. Smith (1992). The Organization of Effective Secondary Schools. *Review of Research in Education, 19,* 171-267.

Lieberman, A., and L. Miller (1981). Synthesis of research on improving schools. *Educational Leadership, 39,* 583-586.

Lieberman, A., and L. Miller (1984). School improvement: Themes and variations. *Teacher's College Record, 86,* 5-18.

Lieberman, A., and M.W. McLaughlin (1992). Networks for educational change: Their power and their problems. *Education Digest, 58,* 4, 63-68.

Liska, A., and M. Reed (1985). Ties to conventional institutions and delinquency: estimating reciprocal effects. *American Sociological Review, 50,* 547-560.

Little, J.W. (1985). Contested ground: The basis of teacher leadership in two restructuring high schools. *The Elementary School Journal, 96,* 1, 47-63.

Little, J.W. (1990). The persistence of privacy: Autonomy and interaction in professional relations. *Teachers College Record, 91*(4), 509-536.

McDermott, J. (1980). High anxiety: Fear of crime in secondary schools. *Contemporary Education* 52: 18-23.

McLaughlin, M.W. (1990). The Rand change agent study revisited: macro perspectives and micro realities. *Educational Researcher, 19,* 11-16.

McMillan, D.W., and D.M. Chavis (1986). Sense of community: A definition and theory. *Journal of Community Psychology, 14,* 6-23.

Miethe, T.D., and R.F. Meier (1994). *Crime and its social context: Toward an integrated theory of offenders, victims, and situations.* Albany, NY: SUNY Press.

Morenoff, J.D., R.J. Sampson, and S. W. Raudenbush (2001). Neighborhood inequality, collective efficacy, and the spatial dynamics of urban violence. *Criminology, 39,* 3, 517-560.

Najaka, S.S., D.C. Gottfredson, and D.B. Wilson (2001). A meta-analytic inquiry into the relationship between selected risk factors and problem behavior. *Prevention Science 2*(4): 257-271.

National Institute of Education (1978). *Violent schools – safe schools: The Safe School Study report to Congress (Vol I).* Washington, DC: U.S. Government Printing Office.

National School Safety Center (2001). *School Associated Violent Deaths.* CA: National School Safety Center.

Newmann, F.M. (1981). Reducing student alienation in high schools: Implications of theory. *Harvard Educational Review, 51,* 546-564.

Newmann, F.M. (1996). Center on Organization and Restructuring of Schools: Activities and Accomplishments, 1990-1996 Final Report. Madison: Center on Organization and Restructuring of Schools, Wisconsin Center for Education Research.

Newmann, F.M., R.A. Rutter, and M.S. Smith (1989). Organizational factors affecting school sense of efficacy, community, and expectations. *Sociology of Education, 62,* 221-238.

Newmann, F.M. and G.G. Wehlage (1995). *Successful school restructuring: A report to the public and educators.* Madison: Center on Organization and Restructuring of Schools, Wisconsin Center for Education Research, University of Wisconsin.

Purkey, S.C, and M.S. Smith (1983). Effective schools: A review. *Elementary School Journal, 83,* 427-452.

Rowan, B. (1990). Commitment and control: Alternative strategies for the organizational design of schools. *Review of Research in Education,* 16, 353-392.

Rutter, M., B. Maughan, P. Mortimore, J. Outson, and A. Smith (1979). *Fifteen thousand hours: Secondary schools and their effects on children.* Cambridge, MA: Harvard University Press.

Sampson, R.J. (1999). What "Community" Supplies. In Fergusen, R.F., and W.T. Dickens (ed) *Urban Problems and Community Development.* Washington, DC: Brookings Institution Press.

Sampson, R.J. (2002). Transcending tradition: New directions in community research, Chicago style. *Criminology,* 40, 2

Sampson, R.J., J.D. Morenoff, and F. Earls (1999). Beyond Spatial Capital: Spatial Dynamics of Collective Efficacy for Children. *American Sociological Review, 64,* p. 633-660.

Sampson, R.J., and S.W. Raudenbush (1999). Assessing Direct and Indirect Effects in Multilevel Designs with Latent Variables. *Sociological Methods and Research, 28, 2,* 123-154.

Sampson, R.J., S.W. Raudenbush, and F. Earls (1997). Neighborhoods and Violent Crime: A Multilevel Study of Collective Efficacy. *Science, 277, 5328,* 918-924.

Schwartz, G., D. Merten, and R.J. Bursik, Jr. (1987). Teaching styles and performance values in junior high school: The impersonal, nonpersonal, and personal. *American Journal of Education, 95,* 346-370.

Shaw, C., and H. McKay (1972). *Delinquency and Urban Areas.* Chicago: University of Chicago Press.

Simonsen, A. A. (1998). *The effects of community disorganization on school administrative practices: Implications for delinquency prevention practice.* Unpublished masters thesis, University of Maryland, College Park.

Solomon, D., V. Battistich, D. Kim, and M. Watson (1997). Teacher practices associated with students' sense of the classroom as a community. *Social Psychology of Education, 1,* 235-267.

Solomon, D., M. Watson, V. Battistich, E. Schaps, and K. Delucchi (1992). Creating a caring community: Educational practices that promote children's prosocial development. In Oser, F.K., A. Dick, and J.L. Patry (eds.), *Effective and responsible teaching: The new synthesis.* San Francisco: Jossey-Bass, pp. 383-396.

Thornberry, T.P. (1987). Toward an interactional theory of delinquency. *Criminology, 25,* 4, p. 863-891.

Thornberry, T.P. (1996). Empirical support for interactional theory: A review of the literature. In J.D. Hawkins (ed.) *Delinquency and Crime: Current Theories.* Cambridge: University Press.

Thornberry, T.P., A.J. Lizotte, M.D. Krohn, M. Farnworth, and S.J. Jang (1991). Testing interactional theory: An examination of reciprocal causal relationships among family, school, and delinquency. *Journal of Criminal Law and Criminology, 82,* 1, 3-35.

Waller, W. (1932). *The Sociology of Teaching.* NY: Russell and Russell.

Welsh, W.N., J.R. Greene, and P.H. Jenkins (1999). School Disorder: The Influence of Individual, Institutional, and Community Factors. *Criminology, 37, 1,* 73-115.

Welsh, W.N. (2000). The Effects of School Climate on School Disorder. *ANNALS of AAPSS*, 567, 88-107.

Werner, E.E., and R.S. Smith (1992). *Overcoming the odds: High risk children from birth to adulthood.* Ithaca, NY: Cornell University Press.

INDEX

50th percentile, x, xi, 76, 102, 103, 104, 105, 106, 107, 108, 109, 110, 111, 112, 113, 114, 115, 116, 117
Absenteeism, 17, 18
Academic achievement, 13, 17, 20, 21, 22, 24, 28, 127, 128, 132
Academic performance, 2, 20, 28, 127, 134
Agnew, R., 5, 25, 26, 136
Alternative schools, xi, 112, 114, 125, 129
Arunkumar, A., 13
Attachment, 14, 16, 17, 23, 24, 25, 26, 27, 28, 29, 30, 49, 51, 63, 122, 130
Bachman, J.G., 63, 122, 141
Battistich, V., 4, 11, 12, 13, 14, 19, 20, 21, 22, 29, 43, 46, 128, 132, 133, 136, 145
Belief, 8, 23, 24, 25, 27, 28, 29, 30, 49, 52, 130
Belonging, 8, 11, 12, 13, 14, 22, 23, 29, 51, 56, 128, 138
Bird, T., 14, 136
Bollen, K.A., 68, 136
Botvin, G.J., 3, 136
Brooks, K., 1, 136
Bryk, A.S., 4, 9, 12, 13, 14, 15, 16, 17, 18, 30, 43, 46, 63, 65, 122, 123, 127, 128, 129, 136, 137, 142
Bursik, R.J., 13, 145
Cantor, D., 2, 140
Capell, F., 13, 140

Census, 38, 67
  divorce rate, 68
  female headed household, 67
  median income, 67
  poverty level, 68, 136
  welfare, 10, 67
Cernkovich, S., 5, 25, 137
Chandler, K.A., 1, 37, 137, 141
Chapman, C.D., 37, 137
Chavis, D.M., 11, 143
Chen, X., 1, 141
Child Development Project, 132, 133
Choy, S.P., 1, 141
Climate, 3, 8, 9, 14, 19, 28, 29, 35, 37, 126, 132, 134, 135, 140
Collaboration, 4, 13, 15, 29, 30, 43, 46, 122, 132, 134, 135
Collective efficacy, 4, 68, 131, 135, 143
Collegiality, 8, 9, 10, 13, 16, 21, 46, 134
Comer, J.P., 132, 137, 140
Commitment, 12, 13, 14, 15, 21, 23, 25, 26, 27, 28, 29, 30, 49, 52, 63, 132, 134
Common agenda, 15, 16, 21, 46, 128
Communal school
  organization, 4, 5, 8, 11, 12, 13, 14, 15, 16, 17, 18, 19, 20, 21, 22, 23, 29, 30, 31, 32, 38, 47, 62, 63, 64, 65,

68, 72, 83, 86, 89, 90, 93,
    94, 97, 119, 120, 121, 122,
    123, 124, 125, 126, 127,
    128, 129, 130, 131, 132,
    133, 134, 135, 136, 137,
    142, 143, 144, 145
collaboration, 4, 13, 15, 29,
    30, 43, 46, 122, 132,
    134, 135
common agenda, 15, 16, 21,
    46, 128
consensus on community,
    43, 47
ethos of caring, 15, 16, 19,
    46, 128
goals and norms, 4, 43, 46,
    123, 128, 129, 130, 131,
    134, 135
involvement, 4, 23, 25, 29,
    46, 49, 55, 127, 128,
    132, 136
shared values, 7, 13, 14, 15,
    18, 19, 46, 128, 134
supportive and collaborative
    relations, 43, 46, 130,
    131
supportive relations, 4, 13,
    15, 21, 133
supportive relationships, 4,
    13, 15, 21, 133
Community, 4, 8, 11, 12, 13,
    14, 15, 16, 18, 19, 20, 22,
    23, 29, 38, 47, 63, 64, 89,
    122, 123, 124, 125, 126,
    127, 128, 129, 130, 131,
    132, 133, 134, 135, 136,
    137, 142, 143, 144, 145
Consensus on community, 43,
    47

Control variables, 22, 62, 68,
    72, 76, 83, 84, 85, 86, 90,
    94, 97, 102, 120, 122
neighborhood crowding, 62,
    83
neighborhood poverty, 62,
    67, 83, 84, 94, 122
percentage male students,
    83, 84, 93
student age, 62, 83
student enrollment, 62, 76,
    77, 83, 84, 86, 94, 97,
    102, 117, 121
student racial heterogeneity,
    62, 67, 76, 77, 83, 85,
    86, 97, 108, 117, 121
student/teacher ratio, 62, 76,
    77, 83, 84, 85, 86, 93,
    94, 97, 112, 117, 120,
    121, 122, 124
teacher racial heterogeneity,
    62, 65, 76, 77, 83, 86,
    94, 97, 102, 104, 108,
    121, 124, 129
Cook, M.S., 132, 137
Cook, T.D., 27, 139
Cooperation, 7, 8, 15
Corcoran, T.B., 8, 11, 137
Correlation, 17, 22, 38, 42, 47,
    54, 59, 62, 65, 66, 67, 68,
    69, 71, 83, 126
Covariance matrix, 69, 70
Crime, 1, 2, 3, 23, 25, 35, 37,
    68, 135, 137, 138, 140, 143
school crime, 1, 2, 25, 37,
    137, 140
school violence, 2, 142
Crosse, S., 2, 140
Cross-sectional data, 20, 22,
    25, 26, 125, 126

Culture, 7, 8, 9, 13, 134
Czeh, E.R., 2, 140
Delinquency, 2, 3, 4, 5, 18, 20,
    22, 23, 24, 25, 26, 27, 28,
    29, 30, 34, 35, 37, 38, 43,
    49, 54, 58, 59, 62, 63, 68,
    112, 117, 120, 121, 122,
    123, 124, 125, 126, 127,
    128, 129, 130, 131, 134,
    135, 139, 140, 141, 142,
    145
Delinquency prevention, 3, 27,
    28, 33, 62, 131, 134, 135,
    137, 139, 140, 145
    Child Development Project,
        132, 133
    PATHE, 28, 134
    School Development
        Program, 132, 137
Delucchi, K., 12, 145
Deviance, 20, 21, 27, 28
Dewey, J., 11, 137
Divorce rate, 68
Driscoll, M.E., 4, 12, 13, 14,
    15, 16, 17, 18, 30, 43, 46,
    63, 65, 122, 123, 127, 128,
    137
Drug use, 20, 28, 34
Duke, D.L., 8, 137
Earls, F., 4, 144
Effective schools, 3, 7, 8, 9,
    10, 11, 12, 13, 14, 20, 21,
    28, 122, 124, 132, 137
Elliot, D.S., 58, 126, 141, 142
Elrod, H.P., 27, 137
Ethos of caring, 15, 16, 19, 46,
    128
Factor analysis, 46, 47, 51, 52,
    54, 55, 58, 67, 69, 119

Faculty, 7, 10, 14, 15, 16, 41,
    43, 47, 67, 77, 83, 86, 90,
    94, 104, 120, 123, 127, 134
Farnworth, M., 5, 25, 145
Farris, E., 37, 141
Federal Bureau of
    Investigation, 63, 122, 137
Female-headed households,
    38, 41, 126
Fight, 2, 56
Fleury, J.K., 1, 141
Friday, P.C., 27, 137
Fullan, M.G., 8, 13, 123, 129,
    130, 134, 138
Gang, 1, 56, 60
Giordano, P., 5, 25, 137
Goals, 4, 8, 10, 11, 12, 13, 14,
    15, 29, 30, 43, 45, 46, 48,
    122, 123, 128, 129, 130,
    131, 134, 135
Goals and norms, 4, 43, 46,
    123, 128, 129, 130, 131,
    134, 135
Goodenow, C., 12, 13, 138
Goodness-of-Fit Index, 86
Gottfredson, D.C., xv, 2, 3, 4,
    7, 18, 25, 27, 28, 30, 43, 44,
    59, 72, 134, 139
Gottfredson, G.D., xv, 2, 7, 27,
    30, 33, 34, 35, 36, 37, 38,
    39, 40, 42, 43, 44, 46, 51,
    52, 55, 59, 62, 72, 125
Graduation, 2
Grant, J., 13, 140
Greene, J.R., 9, 24, 145
Hantman, I., 2, 140
Hargreaves, A., 13, 123, 129,
    130, 134, 138
Harris, 2, 140
Hawley, N.M., 13, 127, 140

Heaviside, S., 37, 141
High school, 14, 24, 33, 35,
    36, 37, 38, 41, 47, 58, 134,
    137, 142, 143, 145
Hirschi, T., 4, 23, 24, 26, 27,
    29, 30, 49, 141
Holland, J.L., 43, 44, 140
Hom, A., 4, 12, 14, 19, 20, 22,
    136
Huizinga, D., 58, 126, 141
Hunt, H.D., 132, 137
Hybl, L.G., 7, 139
Hypothesis, 4, 17, 18, 27, 31,
    72, 86, 90, 93, 97, 117, 121,
    125, 135
Individuality, 123, 124, 130,
    134
Ingersoll, R., 2, 141
Injury, 2
Interaction, x, xi, 5, 7, 9, 15,
    16, 17, 19, 22, 23, 67, 76,
    77, 97, 98, 99, 100, 101,
    102, 103, 104, 105, 106,
    107, 108, 109, 110, 111,
    112, 113, 114, 115, 116,
    117, 121, 124, 143
Interactions, vii, 10, 76, 97
Involvement, 4, 23, 25, 29, 46,
    49, 55, 127, 128, 132, 136
Jang, S.J., 5, 25, 145
Jenkins, P.H., 5, 9, 24, 25, 29,
    141, 145
Johnson, J., 63, 122, 141
Johnston, L.D., 63, 122, 141
Junior high school, 35, 37, 38,
    41, 58, 145
Kaufman, P., 1, 141
Kelloway, E.K., 69, 70, 86,
    141
Kim, D., 4, 11, 12, 136, 145

Krohn, M.D., 5, 25, 141, 145
Kruse, S.D., 14, 142
LaFree, G., xv, 29, 142
Latent variable, 68, 71, 79, 80,
    119
Latent variable model, 69
Laub, J.H., xv, 135, 142
Lauritsen, J.L., 135, 142
Lawrence, R., 2, 139, 142
Lee, V.E., 9, 10, 12, 15, 132,
    142
Legitimacy, 24, 27, 29, 52, 135
Lieberman, A., 8, 142
Liska, A., 5, 25, 26, 142
LISREL, 5, 68, 69, 70, 141
    covariance matrix, 69, 70
    latent variable, 68, 71, 79,
        80, 119
    latent variable model, 69
    measurement model, 69, 71,
        79, 80, 81, 119
    observed indicator, 68, 79,
        80, 81
    Structural equation
        modeling, 47, 54, 68, 69,
        70, 71, 83, 84, 86, 90,
        93, 120
Little, J.W., 14, 27, 134, 136,
    142, 143
Lizotte, A.J., 5, 25, 145
Louis, 2, 140
Louis, K.L., 14, 142
Massey, J.L., 5, 25, 141
Maughan, B., 13, 144
McDermott, J., 2, 143
McKay, H., 4, 145
McLaughlin, M.W., 13, 142,
    143
McMillan, D.W., 11, 143

Measurement model, 69, 71, 79, 80, 81, 119
Measurement scales, 43, 46, 47, 51, 52, 54, 55, 58, 59, 71, 79, 80, 81, 119, 126
Median income, 67
Meier, R.F., 65, 66, 143
Merten, D., 13, 145
Middle school, 25, 35, 36, 37, 38, 41, 58
Miethe, T.D., 65, 66, 143
Miller, A.K., 1, 8, 141, 142
Miller, L., 1, 8, 141, 142
Modification indices, 72, 76, 89
Morale, 4, 8, 17, 18
Morenoff, J.D., 4, 131, 143, 144
Mortimore, P., 13, 144
Murphy, R.F., 132, 137
Najaka, S.S., 3, 28, 139, 143
National Institute of Education, 37, 143
National School Safety Center, 1, 143
National Study of Delinquency Prevention, xv, 33, 37, 39, 40, 44, 46, 51, 52, 55, 140
Neighborhood, 1, 4, 62, 67, 83, 84, 94, 120, 122, 128, 135, 142
  crowding, 62, 83
  poverty, 62, 67, 83, 84, 94, 122
Neighborhood crowding, 62, 83
Neighborhood poverty, 62, 67, 83, 84, 94, 122
Newmann, F.M., 14, 15, 143, 144

Norms, 3, 4, 7, 8, 9, 11, 12, 13, 15, 16, 17, 19, 20, 21, 23, 24, 25, 28, 29, 30, 43, 46, 52, 123, 128, 129, 131, 132, 134, 135
Observed indicator, 68, 79, 80, 81
Orlandi, M.A., 3, 136
Outson, J., 13, 144
Owner-occupied housing, 38
Parental involvement, 127, 128
PATHE, 28, 134
Payne, A.A., 72, 140
Percentage male students, 62, 83, 84, 93
Performance, 2, 3, 20, 28, 45, 46, 48, 127, 134, 136, 145
Peter, K., 1, 141
Physical attack, 2
Planning, 7, 13, 16, 34, 128, 130, 132, 134
Planty, M.G., 1, 141
Poll, 1
Poverty level, 68, 136
Prevention, 3, 27, 28, 33, 62, 131, 137, 139, 140, 145
  Child Development Project, 132, 133
  PATHE, 28, 134
  School Development Program, 132, 137
Principal, 2, 17, 20, 34, 35, 38, 41, 45, 48
Problem behavior, 3, 4, 5, 14, 22, 28, 33, 34, 132, 136, 139, 143
Problem-solving, 7, 14, 16, 130, 133, 134
Property, 2, 55, 56, 57, 60
Property damage, 2, 5, 23

Public, 1, 2, 3, 14, 38, 39, 40,
41, 67, 126, 141, 144
Public assistance, 38, 39, 40,
41, 67, 126
Purkey, S.C., 8, 144
Racial diversity, 76
Racial heterogeneity, 5, 18, 22,
23, 30, 32, 62, 63, 64, 65,
66, 67, 76, 77, 83, 84, 85,
86, 90, 94, 97, 98, 99, 100,
101, 102, 103, 104, 105,
106, 107, 108, 109, 110,
111, 113, 114, 115, 116,
117, 120, 121, 123, 124,
128, 129, 131, 134
Rand, M.R., 1, 37, 137, 141,
143
Raudenbush, S.W., 4, 143, 144
Reed, M., 5, 25, 26, 142
Regression, 26, 83, 97
Response rate, 33, 34, 35, 37,
41, 126
Rowan, B., 144
Rowand, C., 37, 141
R-squared, 86, 89, 90, 93
Ruddy, S.A., 1, 141
Rules, 7, 9, 13, 19, 24, 25, 27,
29, 30, 50, 52, 53, 130, 135
Rural, 33, 34, 35, 36, 37, 38,
39, 40, 41, 42, 58
Rutter, M., 13, 144
Rutter, R.A., 14, 144
Sampson, R.J., 4, 68, 122, 131,
134, 135, 143, 144
Schaps, E., 4, 12, 136, 145
Schinke, S., 3, 136
Schiraldi, V., 1, 136
School
absenteeism, 17, 18

academic achievement, 13,
17, 20, 21, 22, 24, 28,
127, 128, 132
academic performance, 2, 3,
20, 28, 45, 46, 48, 127,
134, 136, 145
administrators, 4, 7, 8, 9,
13, 15, 21, 28, 45, 48,
127, 134
alternative, xi, 112, 114,
125, 129
belonging, 8, 11, 12, 13, 14,
22, 23, 29, 51, 56, 128,
138
climate, 3, 8, 9, 14, 19, 28,
29, 35, 37, 126, 132,
134, 135, 140
collaboration, 4, 13, 15, 29,
30, 43, 46, 122, 132,
134, 135
collegiality, 8, 9, 10, 13, 16,
21, 46, 134
communal school
organization, 4, 5, 8, 11,
12, 13, 14, 15, 16, 17,
18, 19, 20, 21, 22, 23,
29, 30, 31, 32, 38, 47,
62, 63, 64, 65, 68, 72,
83, 86, 89, 90, 93, 94,
97, 119, 120, 121, 122,
123, 124, 125, 126, 127,
128, 129, 130, 131, 132,
133, 134, 135, 136, 137,
142, 143, 144, 145
collaboration, 4, 13, 15,
29, 30, 43, 46, 122,
132, 134, 135
consensus on
community, 43, 47

goals and norms, 4, 43,
46, 123, 128, 129,
130, 131, 134, 135
involvement, 4, 23, 25,
29, 46, 49, 55, 127,
128, 132, 136
supportive and
collaborative
relations, 43, 46, 130,
131
supportive relations, 4,
13, 15, 21, 133
supportive relationships,
4, 13, 15, 21, 133
community, 4, 8, 11, 12, 13,
14, 15, 16, 18, 19, 20,
22, 23, 29, 38, 47, 63,
64, 89, 122, 123, 124,
125, 126, 127, 128, 129,
130, 131, 132, 133, 134,
135, 136, 137, 142, 143,
144, 145
cooperation, 7, 8, 15
crime, 1, 2, 25, 37, 137, 140
culture, 7, 8, 9, 13, 134
delinquency prevention, 3,
27, 28, 33, 62, 131, 137,
139, 140, 145
Child Development
Project, 132, 133
PATHE, 28, 134
School Development
Program, 132, 137
disorder, 2, 3, 5, 27, 30, 31,
32, 59, 62, 63, 68, 72,
76, 83, 86, 89, 90, 93,
94, 96, 97, 104, 108,
112, 119, 121, 122, 124,
127, 131, 134, 135, 138
drug use, 20, 28, 34

educational mission, 2
effective schools, 3, 7, 8, 9,
10, 11, 12, 13, 14, 20,
21, 28, 122, 124, 132,
137
elementary school, 19, 20,
33, 35, 132
faculty, 7, 10, 14, 15, 16,
41, 43, 47, 67, 77, 83,
86, 90, 94, 104, 120,
123, 127, 134
governance, 128, 130, 131
graduation, 2
high school, 14, 24, 33, 35,
36, 37, 38, 41, 47, 58,
134, 137, 142, 143, 145
junior high school, 35, 37,
38, 41, 58, 145
management, 3, 7, 11, 132
middle school, 25, 35, 36,
37, 38, 41, 58
parental involvement, 127,
128
planning, 7, 13, 16, 34, 128,
130, 132, 134
principal, 2, 17, 20, 34, 35,
38, 41, 45, 48
problem behavior, 3, 4, 5,
14, 22, 28, 33, 34, 132,
136, 139, 143
property, 2, 60
racial heterogeneity, 5, 18,
22, 23, 30, 32, 62, 63,
64, 65, 66, 67, 76, 77,
83, 84, 85, 86, 90, 94,
97, 98, 99, 100, 101,
102, 103, 104, 105, 106,
107, 108, 109, 110, 111,
113, 114, 115, 116, 117,

120, 121, 123, 124, 128,
129, 131, 134
rules, 7, 9, 13, 19, 24, 25,
27, 29, 30, 50, 52, 53,
130, 135
safety, 33, 34, 59
school crime, 1, 2, 25, 37,
137, 140
school violence, 2, 142
school-related deaths, 1
secondary school, 2, 35, 36,
37, 137, 143
sense of community, 11, 14,
19, 20, 22, 122, 125,
127, 129
size, 5, 17, 18, 22, 23, 30,
32, 42, 62, 63, 64, 76,
77, 83, 84, 86, 90, 94,
97, 98, 99, 100, 101,
102, 103, 105, 106, 107,
109, 110, 111, 113, 114,
115, 116, 117, 121, 122
social organization, 3, 4, 7,
8, 9, 10, 15, 21, 30, 31,
43, 123, 124
staff, 8, 9, 10, 14, 18, 132,
134
student, 1, 2, 3, 4, 5, 7, 8, 9,
10, 11, 12, 13, 14, 15,
16, 17, 18, 19, 20, 21,
22, 23, 24, 25, 26, 27,
28, 29, 30, 31, 35, 36,
37, 38, 39, 40, 41, 42,
43, 49, 50, 51, 52, 53,
54, 56, 57, 58, 59, 60,
62, 63, 64, 65, 66, 67,
68, 72, 76, 77, 83, 84,
85, 86, 89, 90, 93, 94,
96, 97, 102, 103, 105,
106, 107, 108, 109, 110,

111, 112, 113, 114, 115,
116, 117, 120, 121, 122,
123, 124, 125, 127, 128,
129, 130, 131, 132, 133,
134, 135, 136, 137, 138,
143, 145
achievement, 5, 14, 28
age, 62, 83
delinquency, 3, 4, 18, 22,
37, 54, 59
enrollment, 5, 17, 18, 22,
23, 30, 32, 42, 62, 63,
64, 76, 77, 83, 84, 86,
90, 94, 97, 98, 99,
100, 101, 102, 103,
105, 106, 107, 109,
110, 111, 113, 114,
115, 116, 117, 121,
122
racial heterogeneity, 62,
63, 64, 67, 76, 77, 83,
85, 86, 94, 97, 98, 99,
100, 101, 103, 105,
106, 107, 108, 109,
110, 111, 113, 114,
115, 116, 117, 121
victimization, 7, 27, 35,
54, 58, 59, 68, 117,
122, 128
student attendance, 2, 3, 13,
25, 28
student bonding, 3, 4, 5, 22,
25, 26, 27, 28, 29, 30,
31, 49, 62, 63, 68, 72,
83, 90, 93, 94, 96, 120,
121, 122, 124, 125, 127,
128, 129, 130, 131, 134,
135
student/teacher ratio, 62, 76,
77, 83, 84, 85, 86, 93,

94, 97, 112, 117, 120,
121, 122, 124
teacher, 2, 3, 4, 7, 8, 9, 10,
11, 12, 13, 14, 15, 16,
17, 19, 20, 21, 23, 24,
25, 27, 28, 36, 37, 38,
41, 43, 45, 46, 48, 50,
51, 53, 54, 55, 56, 58,
59, 62, 63, 64, 65, 67,
68, 76, 77, 83, 84, 85,
86, 89, 93, 94, 96, 97,
98, 99, 100, 101, 102,
103, 104, 105, 106, 107,
108, 109, 110, 111, 112,
113, 114, 115, 116, 117,
120, 121, 122, 124, 128,
129, 130, 132, 133, 134,
135, 137, 141, 142
efficacy, 14, 17, 18, 20,
132
morale, 4, 7
racial heterogeneity, 62,
63, 64, 65, 76, 77, 83,
84, 86, 90, 94, 97, 98,
99, 100, 101, 102,
103, 104, 105, 106,
107, 108, 109, 110,
111, 113, 114, 115,
116, 117, 121, 124,
129
satisfaction, 14, 16, 17,
18, 20, 132
victimization, 37, 54, 55,
58, 59, 68, 89, 96,
104, 120, 122, 124,
128
work enjoyment, 17, 18,
20
teacher turnover, 2

Teacher-administrator
communication, 7
truancy, 17, 21, 133
values, 4, 7, 8, 9, 11, 12, 13,
14, 15, 16, 18, 19, 20,
21, 29, 43, 46, 47, 70,
79, 80, 81, 89, 96, 104,
108, 122, 123, 124, 128,
129, 132, 133, 135, 145
violence, 2, 142
vocational school, 38, 41,
129
School Development Program,
132, 137
School disorder, 2, 3, 5, 27, 30,
31, 32, 59, 62, 63, 68, 72,
76, 83, 86, 89, 90, 93, 94,
96, 97, 104, 108, 112, 119,
121, 122, 124, 127, 131,
134, 135, 138
School safety, 33, 34, 59
School size, 5, 17, 18, 22, 23,
30, 32, 42, 62, 63, 64, 76,
77, 83, 84, 86, 90, 94, 97,
98, 99, 100, 101, 102, 103,
105, 106, 107, 109, 110,
111, 113, 114, 115, 116,
117, 121, 122
School-based interventions, 3,
131, 134, 135
Schools
communal school
organization, 4, 11, 22,
30
personal-communal, 10
rational-bureaucratic, 10, 11
Schwartz, G., 13, 132, 145
Self-report data, 25, 26, 54, 58,
59
validity, 38, 58, 59

Self-selection, 38
Sense of community, 11, 14,
    19, 20, 22, 122, 125, 127,
    129
Shared values, 7, 13, 14, 15,
    18, 19, 46, 128, 134
Shaw, C., 4, 145
Simonsen, A.A., 67, 145
Smith, A., 13, 144
Smith, J.B., 9, 12, 15, 142
Smith, M.S., 8, 14, 144
Smith, R.S., 13, 146
Social bond, 23, 24, 29, 49,
    141
    attachment, 14, 16, 17, 23,
        24, 25, 26, 27, 28, 29,
        30, 49, 51, 63, 122, 130
    belief, 8, 23, 24, 25, 27, 28,
        29, 30, 49, 52, 130
    commitment, 12, 13, 14, 15,
        21, 23, 25, 26, 27, 28,
        29, 30, 49, 52, 63, 132,
        134
    involvement, 4, 23, 25, 29,
        46, 49, 55, 127, 128,
        132, 136
Social control, 4, 23, 24, 27,
    29, 49, 131, 135, 141
    attachment, 14, 16, 17, 23,
        24, 25, 26, 27, 28, 29,
        30, 49, 51, 63, 122, 130
    belief, 8, 23, 24, 25, 27, 28,
        29, 30, 49, 52, 130
    commitment, 12, 13, 14, 15,
        21, 23, 25, 26, 27, 28,
        29, 30, 49, 52, 63, 132,
        134
    involvement, 4, 23, 25, 29,
        46, 49, 55, 127, 128,
        132, 136

Social disorganization, 4, 68
    collective efficacy, 4, 68,
        131, 135, 143
Social organization, 3, 4, 7, 8,
    9, 10, 15, 21, 30, 31, 43,
    123, 124
Solomon, D., 4, 11, 12, 13, 19,
    29, 43, 46, 136, 145
Staff, 8, 9, 10, 14, 18, 132, 134
Standardized residuals, 72, 76,
    89
Statistical weighting, 42
Structural equation modeling,
    47, 54, 68, 69, 70, 71, 83,
    84, 86, 90, 93, 120
    covariance matrix, 69, 70
    Goodness-of-Fit Index, 86
    identification, 69
    latent variable, 68, 71, 79,
        80, 119
    latent variable model, 69
    LISREL, 5, 68, 69, 70, 141
    measurement model, 69, 71,
        79, 80, 81, 119
    model estimation, 69
    model respecification, 69,
        70
    model specification, 69
    modification indices, 72,
        76, 89
    observed indicator, 68, 79,
        80, 81
    R-squared, 86, 89, 90, 93
    standardized residuals, 72,
        76, 89
    testing of fit, 69
Student, 1, 2, 3, 4, 5, 7, 8, 9,
    10, 11, 12, 13, 14, 15, 16,
    17, 18, 19, 20, 21, 22, 23,
    24, 25, 26, 27, 28, 29, 30,

31, 35, 36, 37, 38, 39, 40,
41, 42, 43, 49, 50, 51, 52,
53, 54, 56, 57, 58, 59, 60,
62, 63, 64, 65, 66, 67, 68,
72, 76, 77, 83, 84, 85, 86,
89, 90, 93, 94, 96, 97, 102,
103, 105, 106, 107, 108,
109, 110, 111, 112, 113,
114, 115, 116, 117, 120,
121, 122, 123, 124, 125,
127, 128, 129, 130, 131,
132, 133, 134, 135, 136,
137, 138, 143, 145
achievement, 5, 14, 28
age, 62, 83
bonding, 3, 4, 5, 22, 25, 26,
27, 28, 29, 30, 31, 49,
62, 63, 68, 72, 83, 90,
93, 94, 96, 120, 121,
122, 124, 125, 127, 128,
129, 130, 131, 134, 135
delinquency, 3, 4, 18, 22,
37, 54, 59
non-white, 41, 42
racial heterogeneity, 62, 63,
64, 67, 76, 77, 83, 85,
86, 94, 97, 98, 99, 100,
101, 103, 105, 106, 107,
108, 109, 110, 111, 113,
114, 115, 116, 117, 121
student/teacher ratio, 62, 76,
77, 83, 84, 85, 86, 93,
94, 97, 112, 117, 120,
121, 122, 124
truancy, 17, 21, 133
victimization, 7, 27, 35, 54,
58, 59, 68, 117, 122, 128
Student achievement, 5, 14, 28
Student age, 62, 83

Student bond, 3, 4, 5, 22, 25,
26, 27, 28, 29, 30, 31, 49,
62, 63, 68, 72, 83, 90, 93,
94, 96, 120, 121, 122, 124,
125, 127, 128, 129, 130,
131, 134, 135
Student bonding, 3, 5, 22, 25,
26, 27, 28, 29, 30, 31, 49,
62, 63, 68, 72, 83, 90, 93,
94, 96, 120, 121, 122, 124,
125, 127, 128, 129, 130,
131, 134, 135
attachment, 14, 16, 17, 23,
24, 25, 26, 27, 28, 29,
30, 49, 51, 63, 122, 130
belief, 8, 23, 24, 25, 27, 28,
29, 30, 49, 52, 130
commitment, 12, 13, 14, 15,
21, 23, 25, 26, 27, 28,
29, 30, 49, 52, 63, 132,
134
involvement, 4, 23, 25, 29,
46, 49, 55, 127, 128,
132, 136
Student delinquency, 3, 4, 18,
22, 37, 54, 59
Student enrollment, 5, 17, 18,
22, 23, 30, 32, 42, 62, 63,
64, 76, 77, 83, 84, 86, 90,
94, 97, 98, 99, 100, 101,
102, 103, 105, 106, 107,
109, 110, 111, 113, 114,
115, 116, 117, 121, 122
Student victimization, 7, 27,
35, 54, 58, 59, 68, 117, 122,
128
Student/teacher ratio, 62, 76,
77, 83, 84, 85, 86, 93, 94,
97, 112, 117, 120, 121, 122,
124

Suburban, 19, 33, 35, 36, 37,
41, 42, 58
Supportive and collaborative
relations, 43, 46, 130, 131
Supportive relationships, 4, 13,
15, 21, 133
Survey, 1, 2, 33, 34, 35, 37, 38,
41, 54, 122, 125, 126
Taylor, B.M., 37, 137
Teacher, 2, 3, 4, 7, 8, 9, 10, 11,
12, 13, 14, 15, 16, 17, 19,
20, 21, 23, 24, 25, 27, 28,
36, 37, 38, 41, 43, 45, 46,
48, 50, 51, 53, 54, 55, 56,
58, 59, 62, 63, 64, 65, 67,
68, 76, 77, 83, 84, 85, 86,
89, 93, 94, 96, 97, 98, 99,
100, 101, 102, 103, 104,
105, 106, 107, 108, 109,
110, 111, 112, 113, 114,
115, 116, 117, 120, 121,
122, 124, 128, 129, 130,
132, 133, 134, 135, 137,
141, 142
efficacy, 14, 17, 18, 20, 132
morale, 4, 7
non-white, 41
racial heterogeneity, 62, 63,
64, 65, 76, 77, 83, 84,
86, 90, 94, 97, 98, 99,
100, 101, 102, 103, 104,
105, 106, 107, 108, 109,
110, 111, 113, 114, 115,
116, 117, 121, 124, 129
satisfaction, 14, 16, 17, 18,
20, 132
student/teacher ratio, 62, 76,
77, 83, 84, 85, 86, 93,
94, 97, 112, 117, 120,
121, 122, 124

turnover, 2
victimization, 37, 54, 55,
58, 59, 68, 89, 96, 104,
120, 122, 124, 128
work enjoyment, 17, 18, 20
Teacher morale, 4, 7
Teacher turnover, 2
Teacher-administrator
communication, 7
Theft, 2, 21, 26, 133
Thornberry, T.P., 5, 25, 26,
145
Thum, Y.M., 15, 137
Truancy, 17, 21, 133
t-test, 102, 104, 108, 112, 117
Unemployment, 38, 39, 40, 41,
68
Urban, 2, 33, 34, 35, 36, 37,
38, 39, 40, 41, 42, 58, 126,
128, 142, 143
Values, 4, 7, 8, 9, 11, 12, 13,
14, 15, 16, 18, 19, 20, 21,
29, 43, 46, 47, 70, 79, 80,
81, 89, 96, 104, 108, 122,
123, 124, 128, 129, 132,
133, 135, 145
Victimization, 1, 2, 5, 7, 22,
27, 29, 30, 35, 37, 38, 43,
54, 55, 58, 59, 62, 63, 68,
89, 96, 104, 117, 120, 122,
123, 124, 125, 127, 128,
129, 130, 131, 135
Violence, 1, 2, 26, 142, 143
school violence, 2, 142
Vocational school, 38, 41, 129
Waller, W., 7, 145
Watson, M., 4, 11, 12, 136,
145
Weapon, 1, 2, 21, 56, 57, 60,
61, 133

Wehlage, G.G., 14, 144
Welfare, 10, 67
Welsh, W.N., 5, 9, 24, 25, 29, 128, 139, 145, 146

Werner, E.E., 13, 146
Williams, C., 37, 141, 142
Wilson, D.B., 3, 28, 139, 143
Ziedenberg, J., 1, 136